THE PICTURE BOOK OF

BRIDES

SUNNY STREET
BOOKS

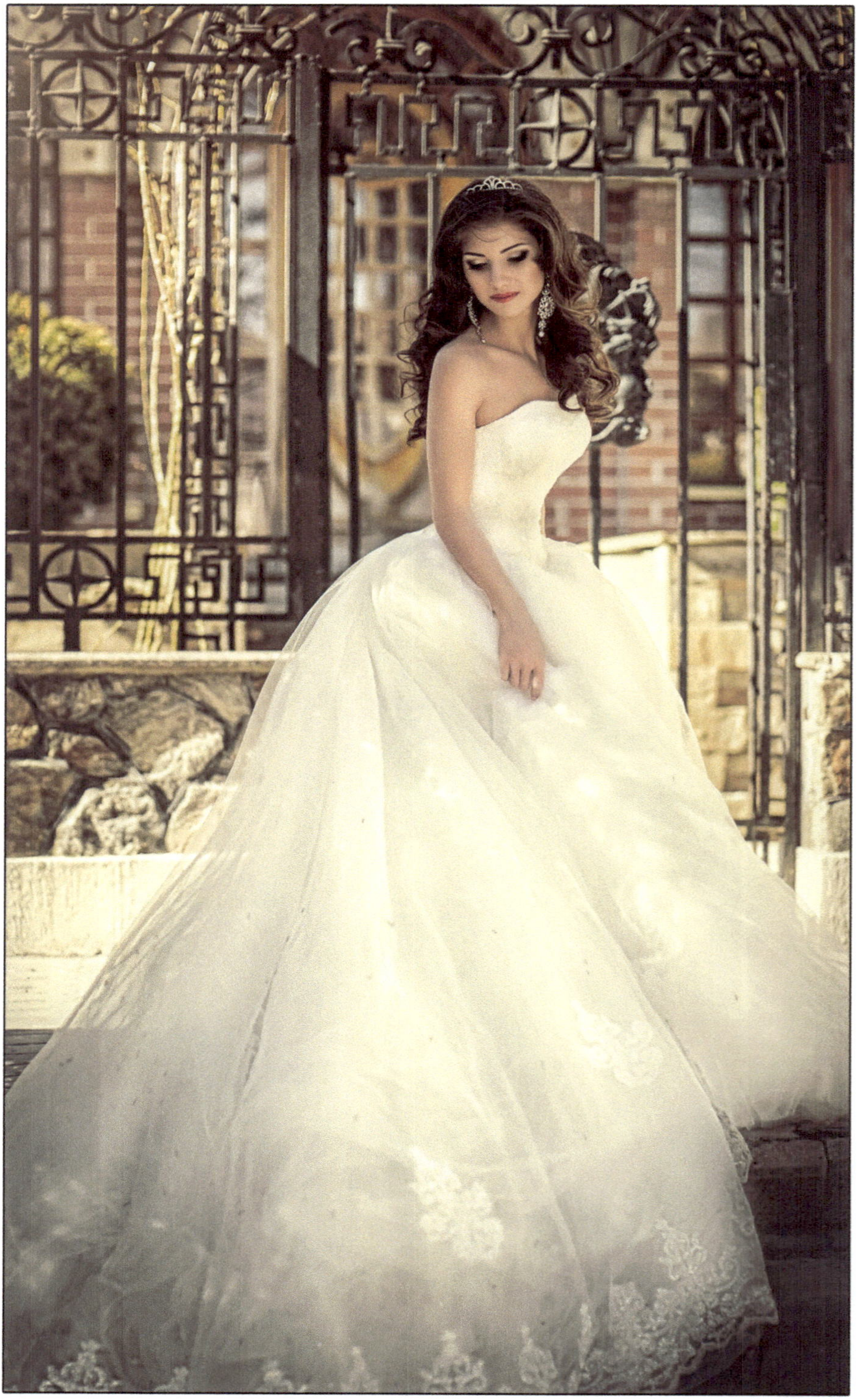

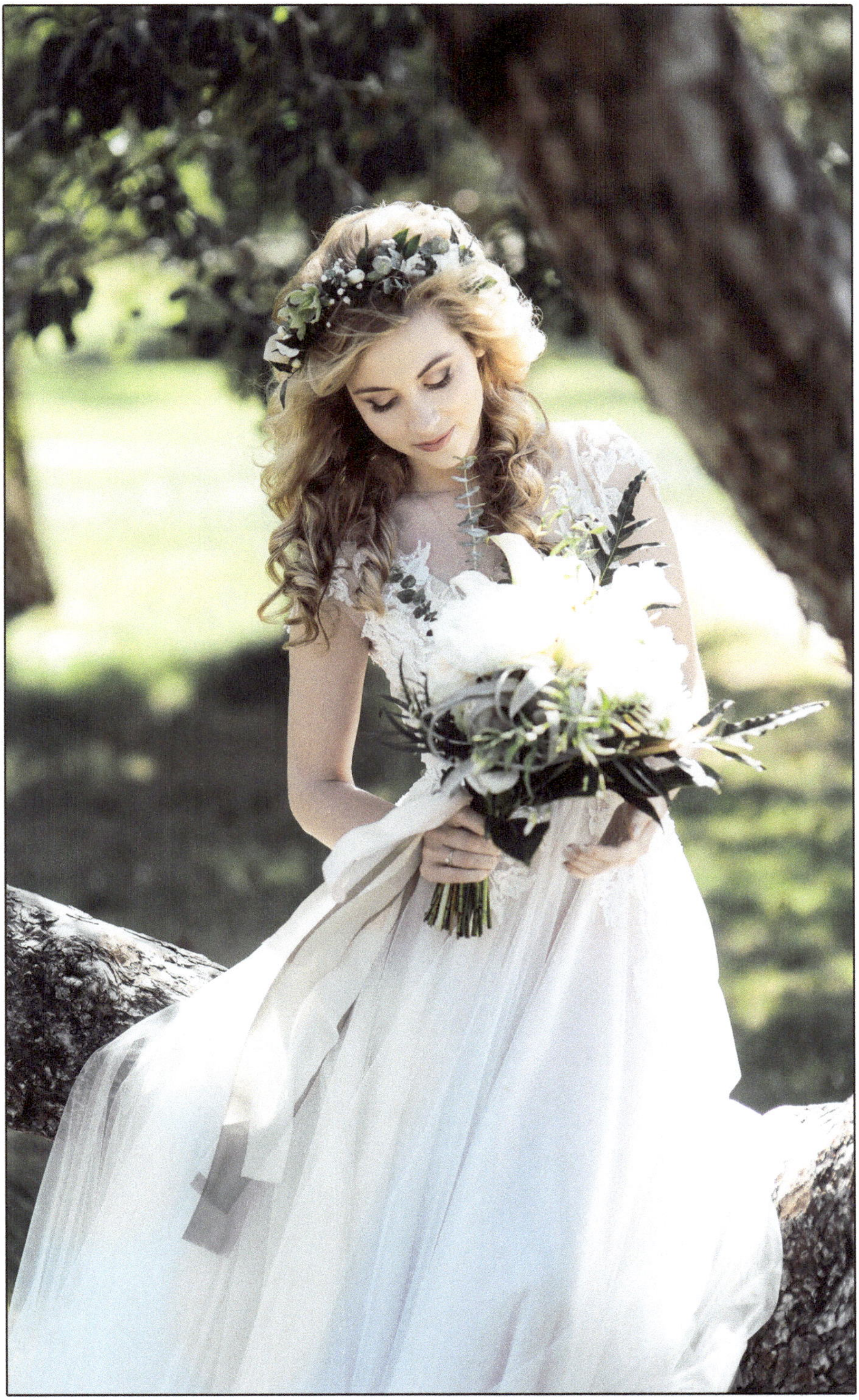

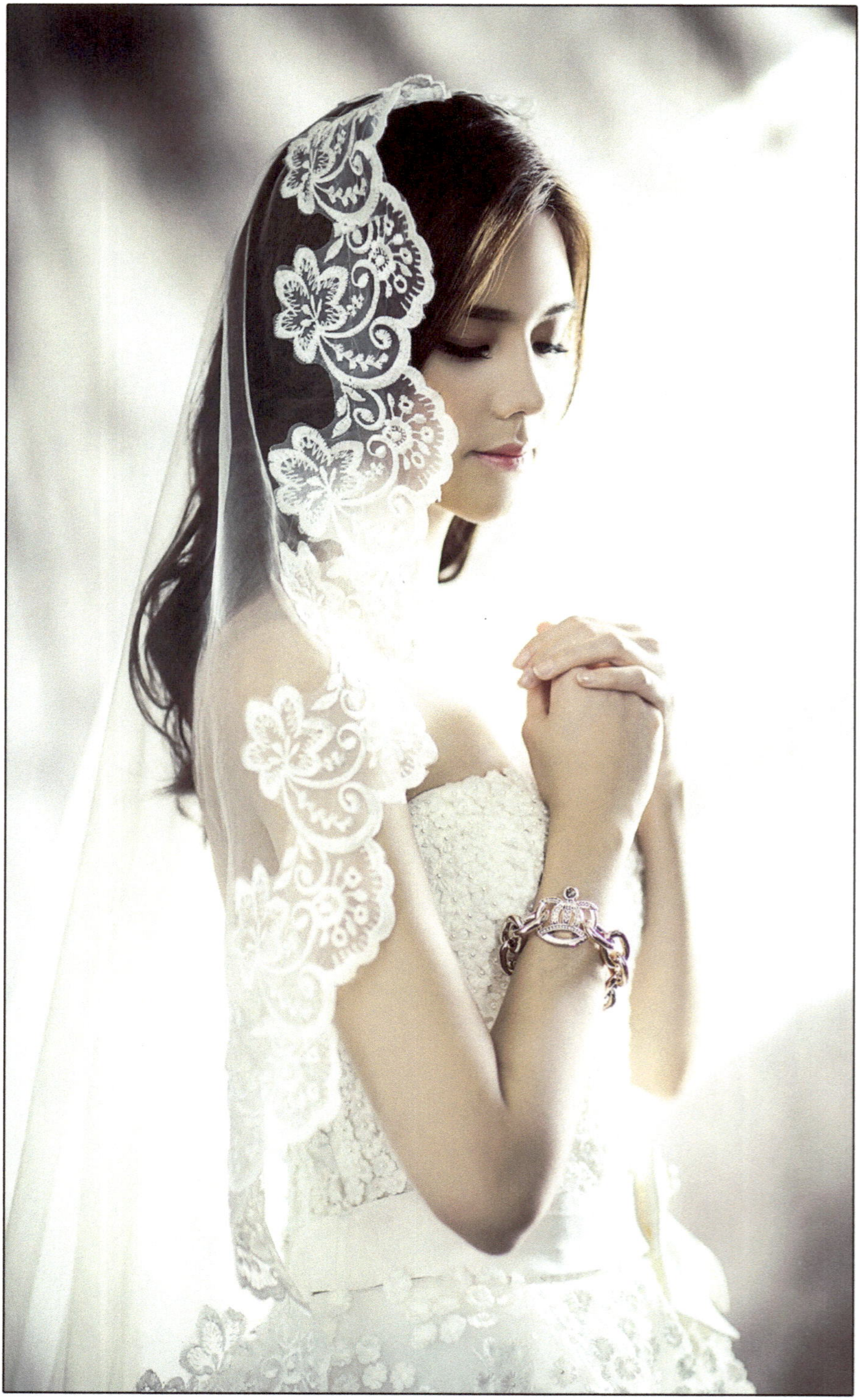

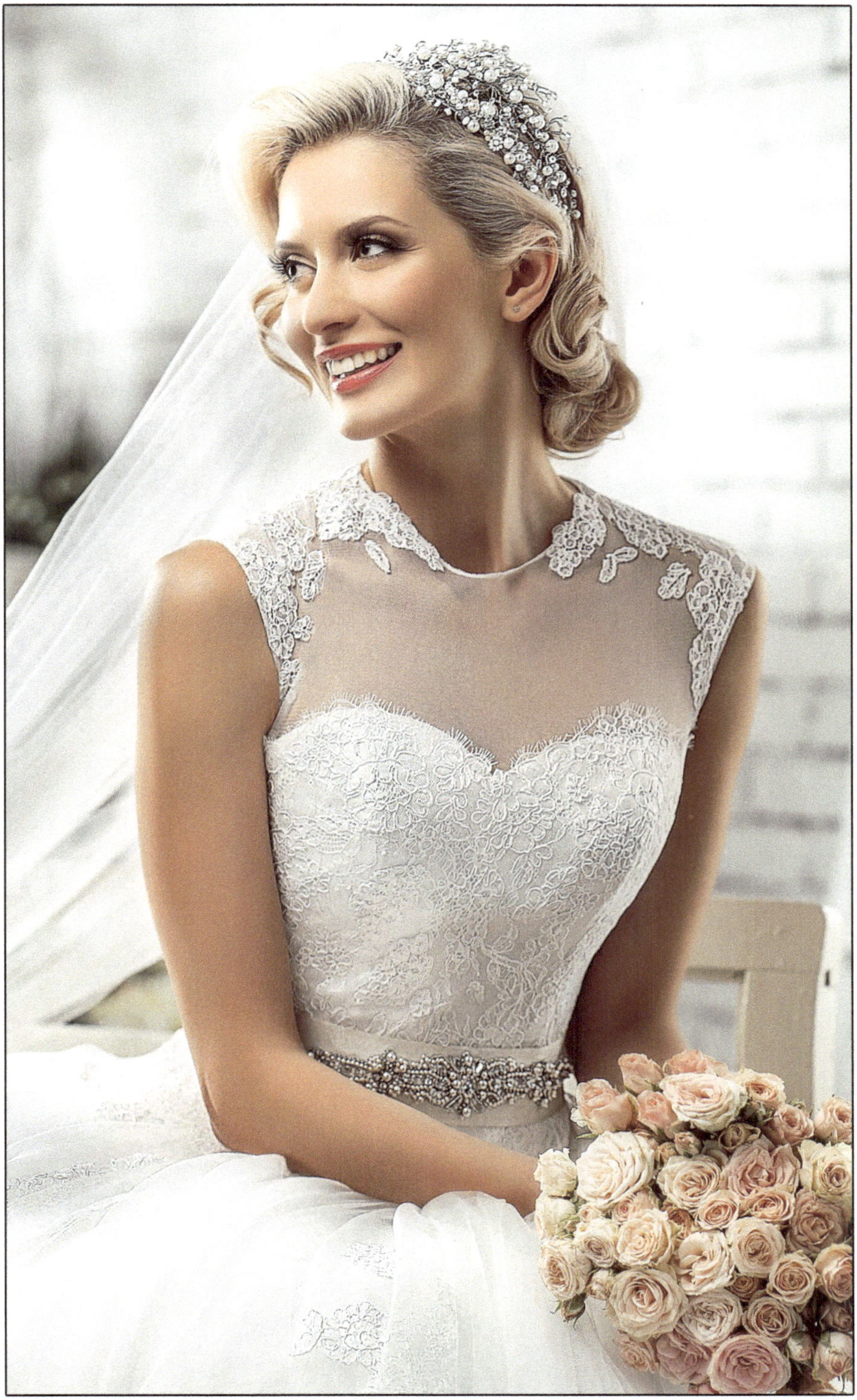

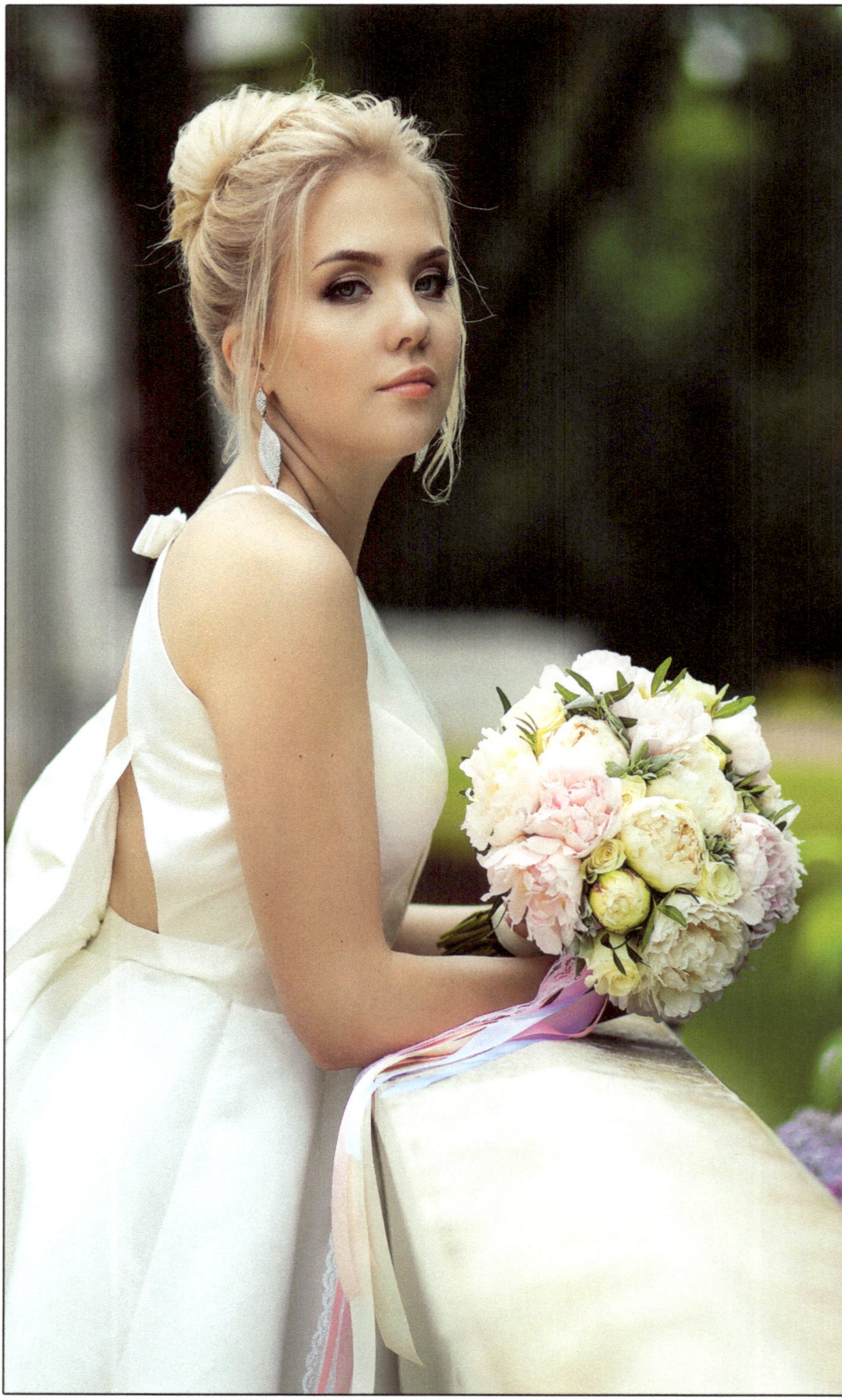

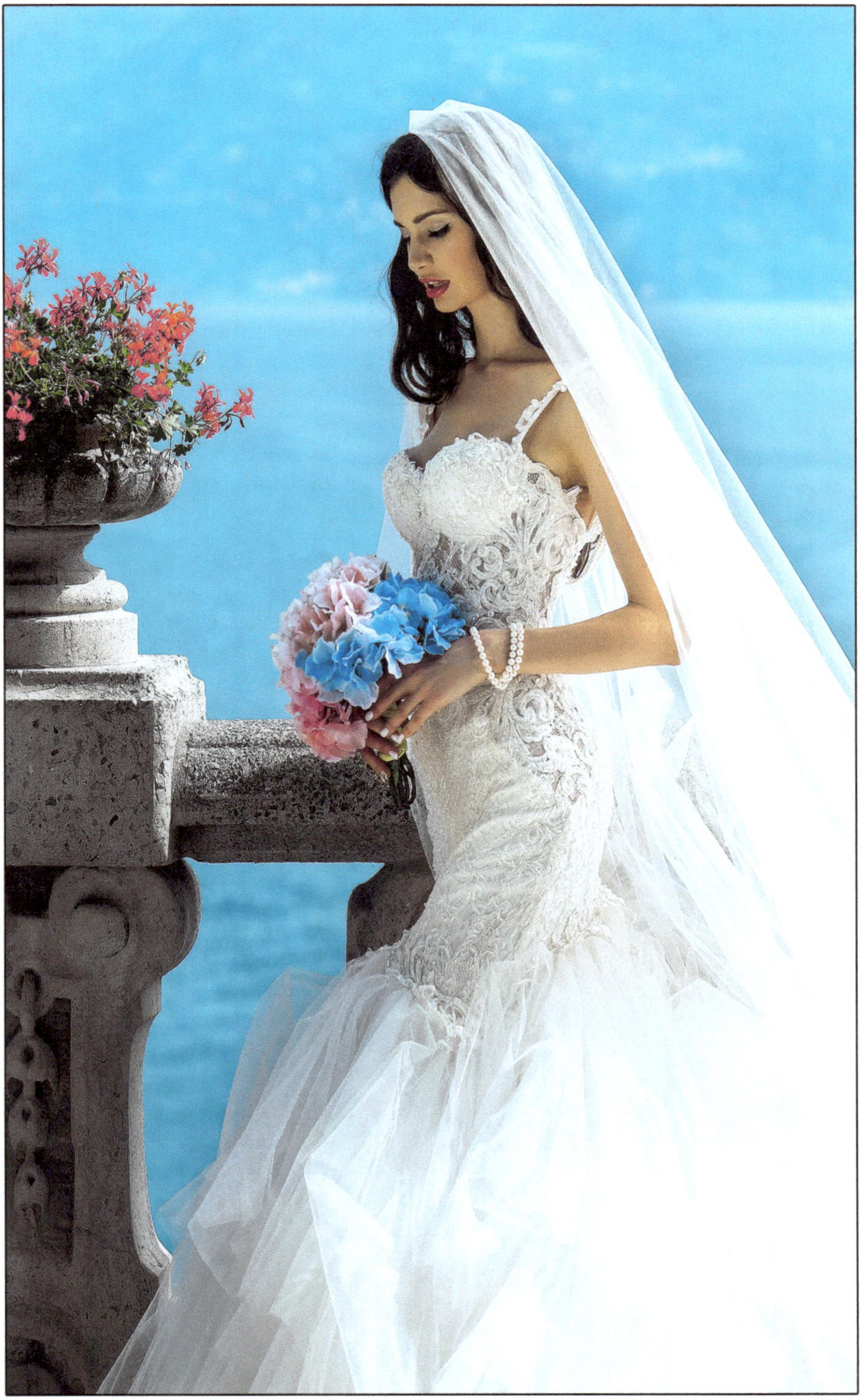

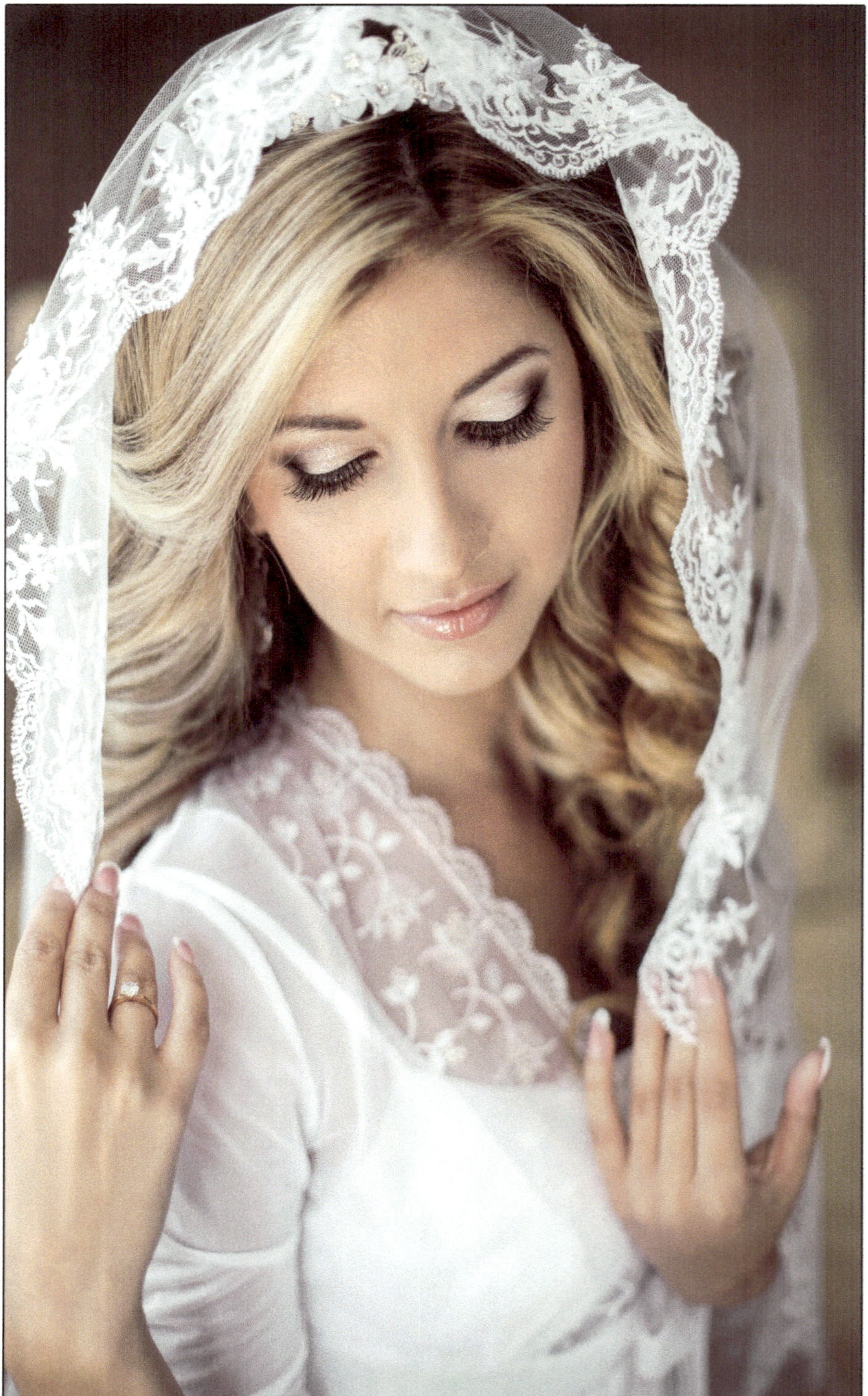

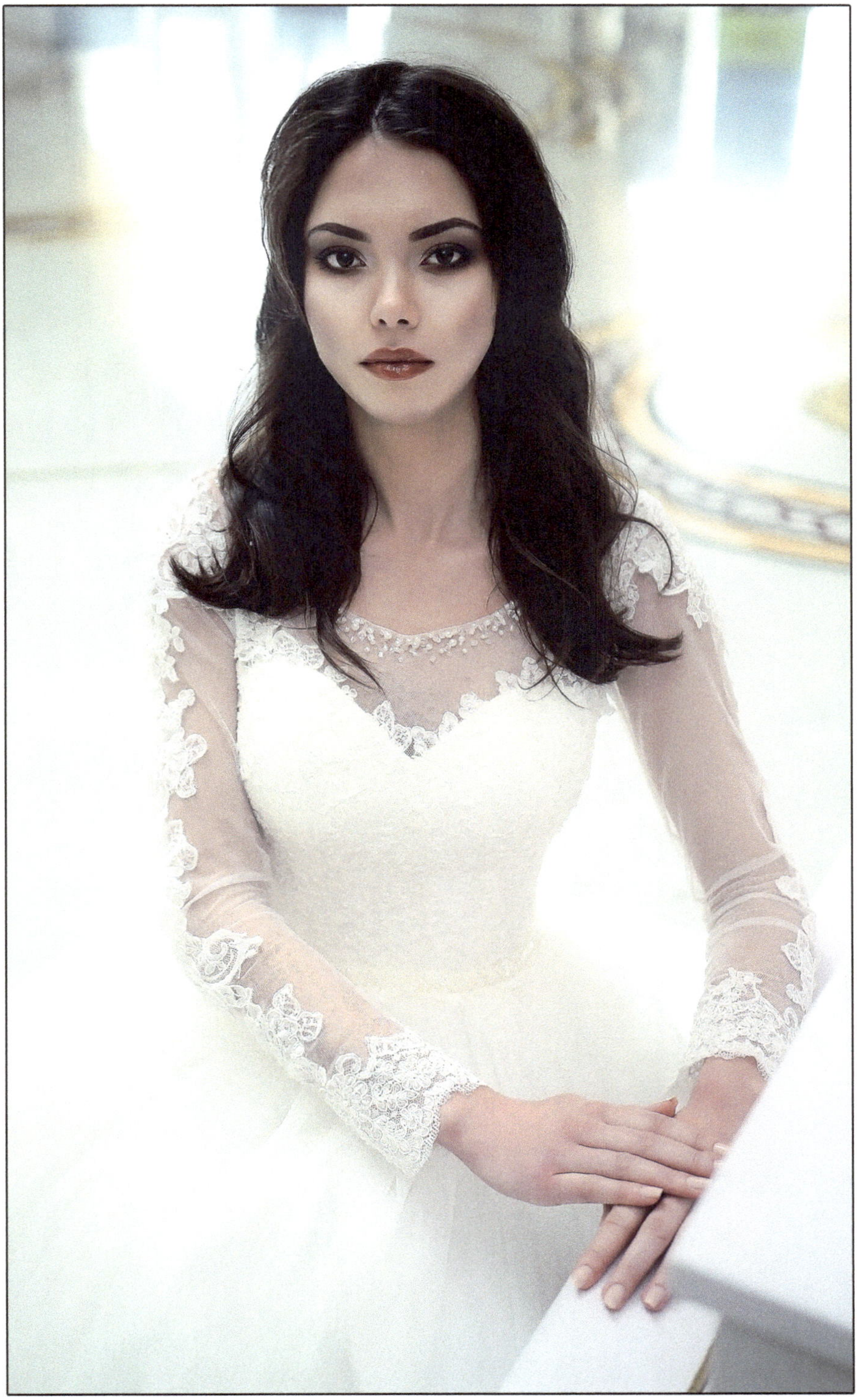

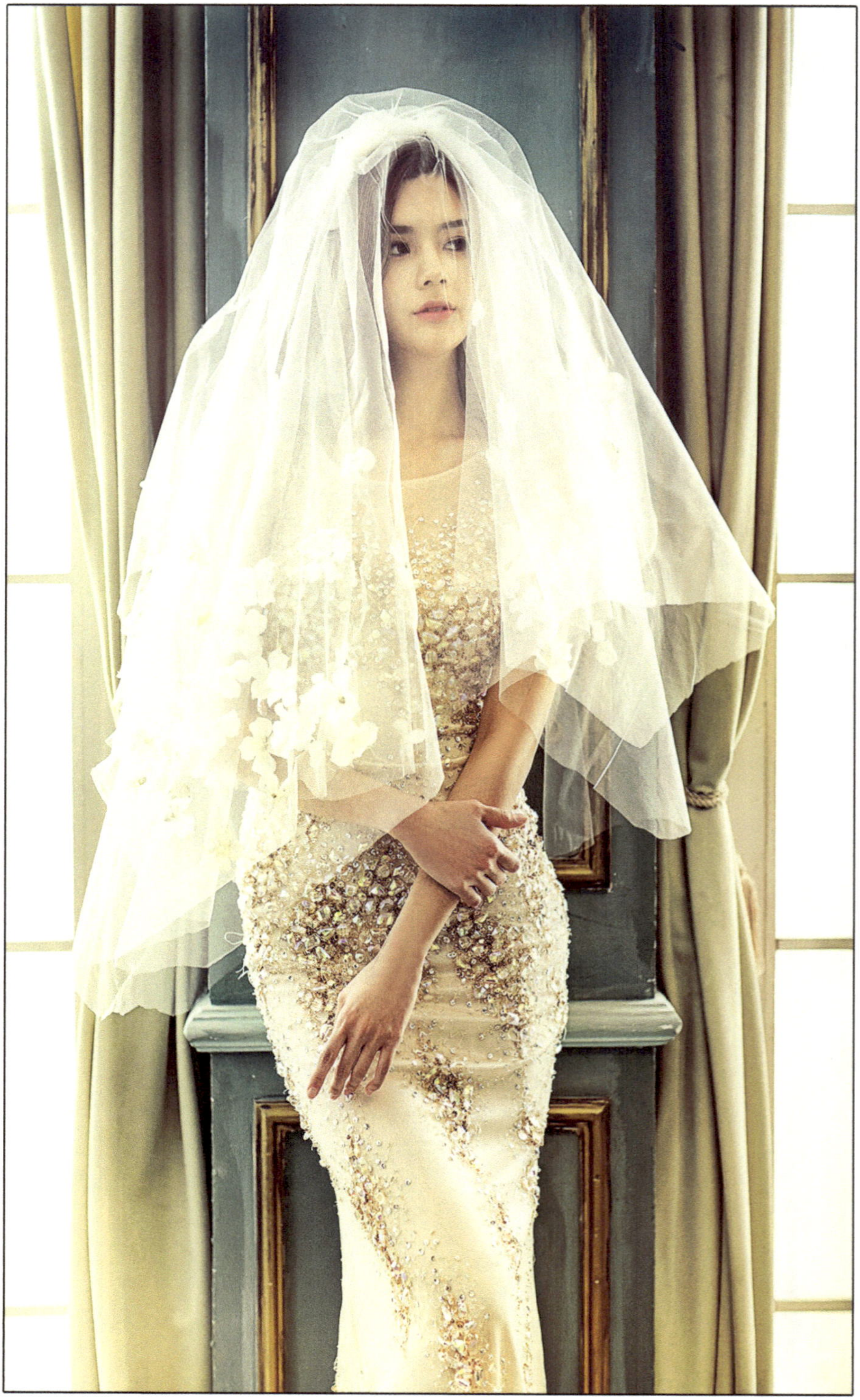

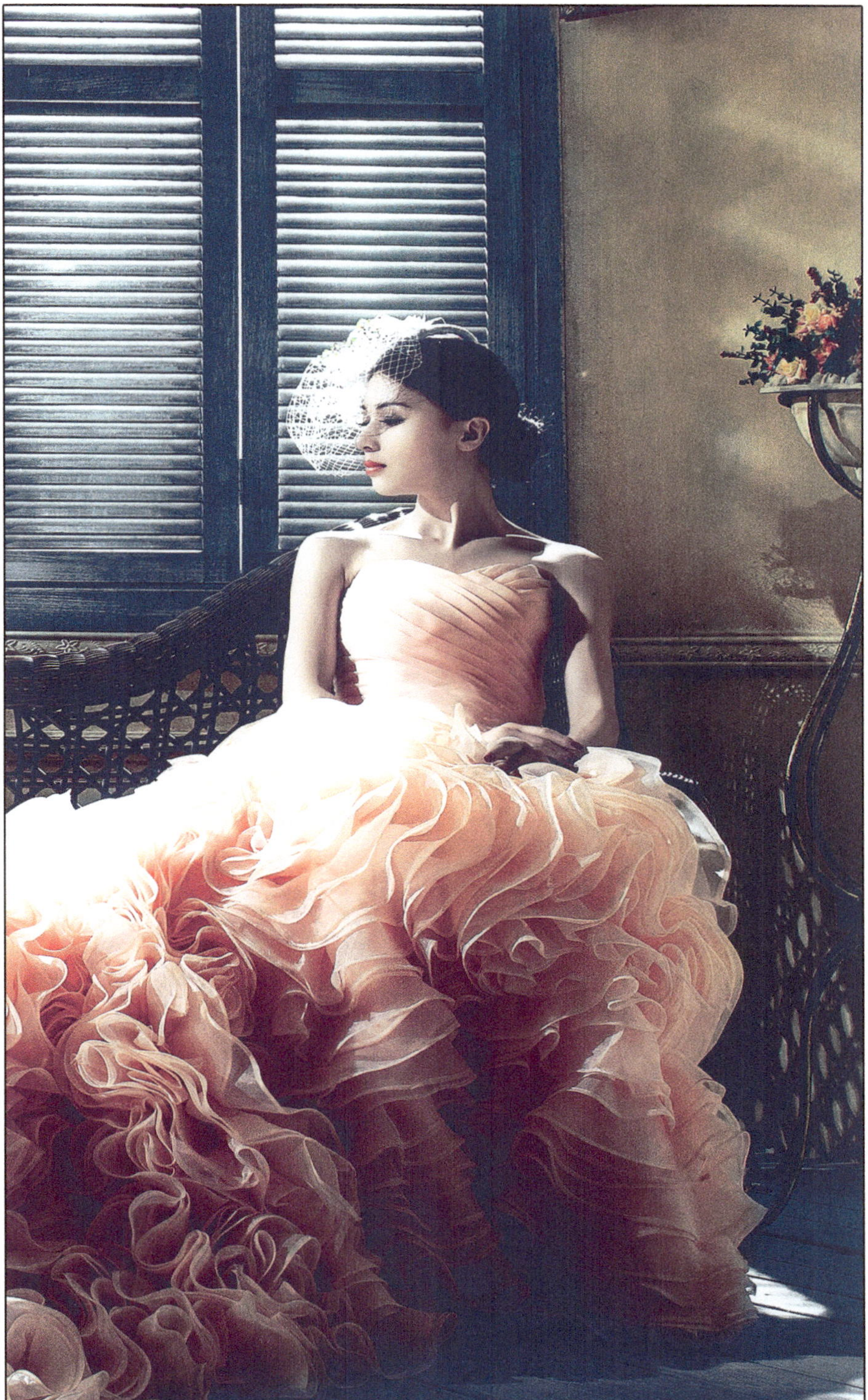

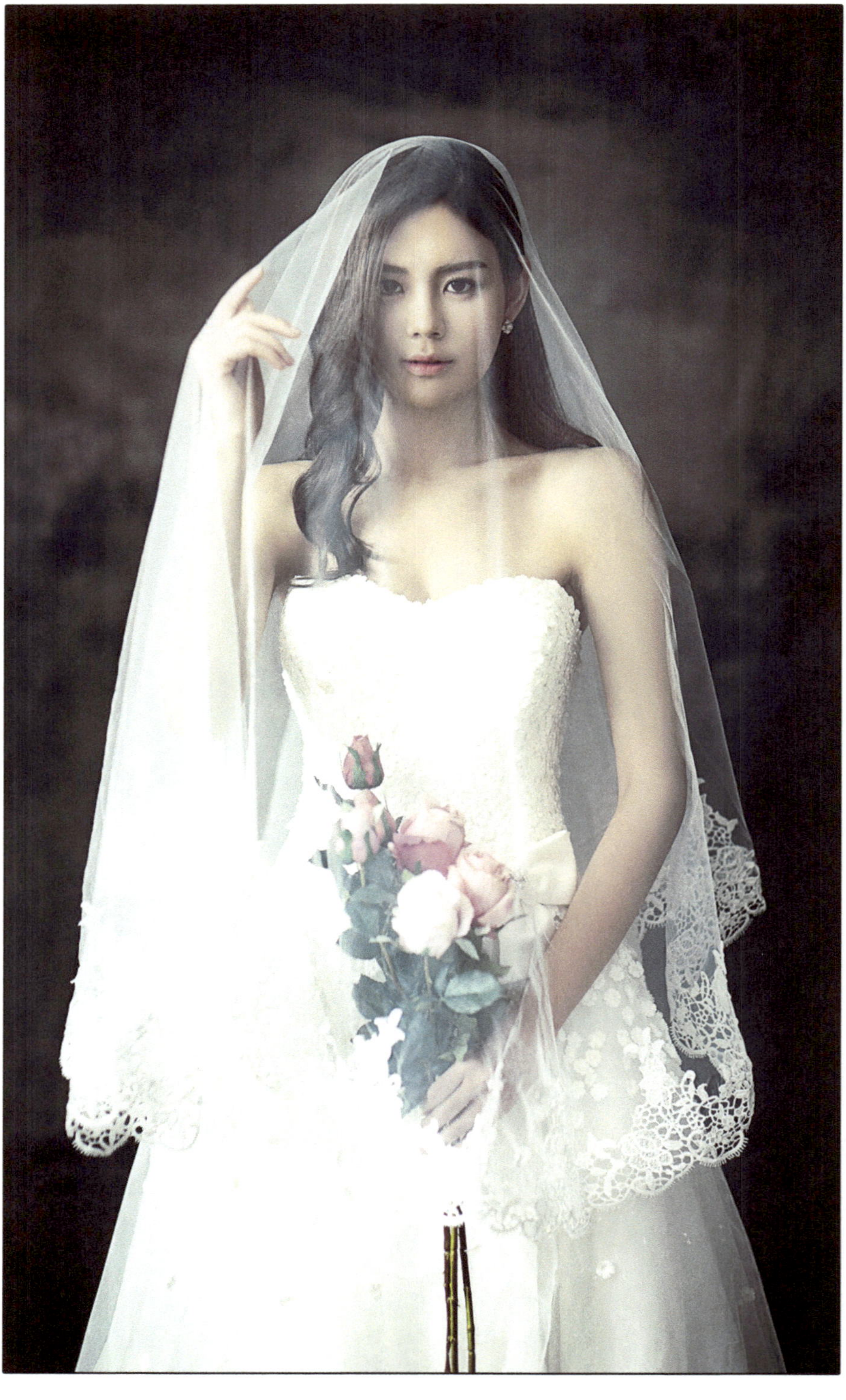

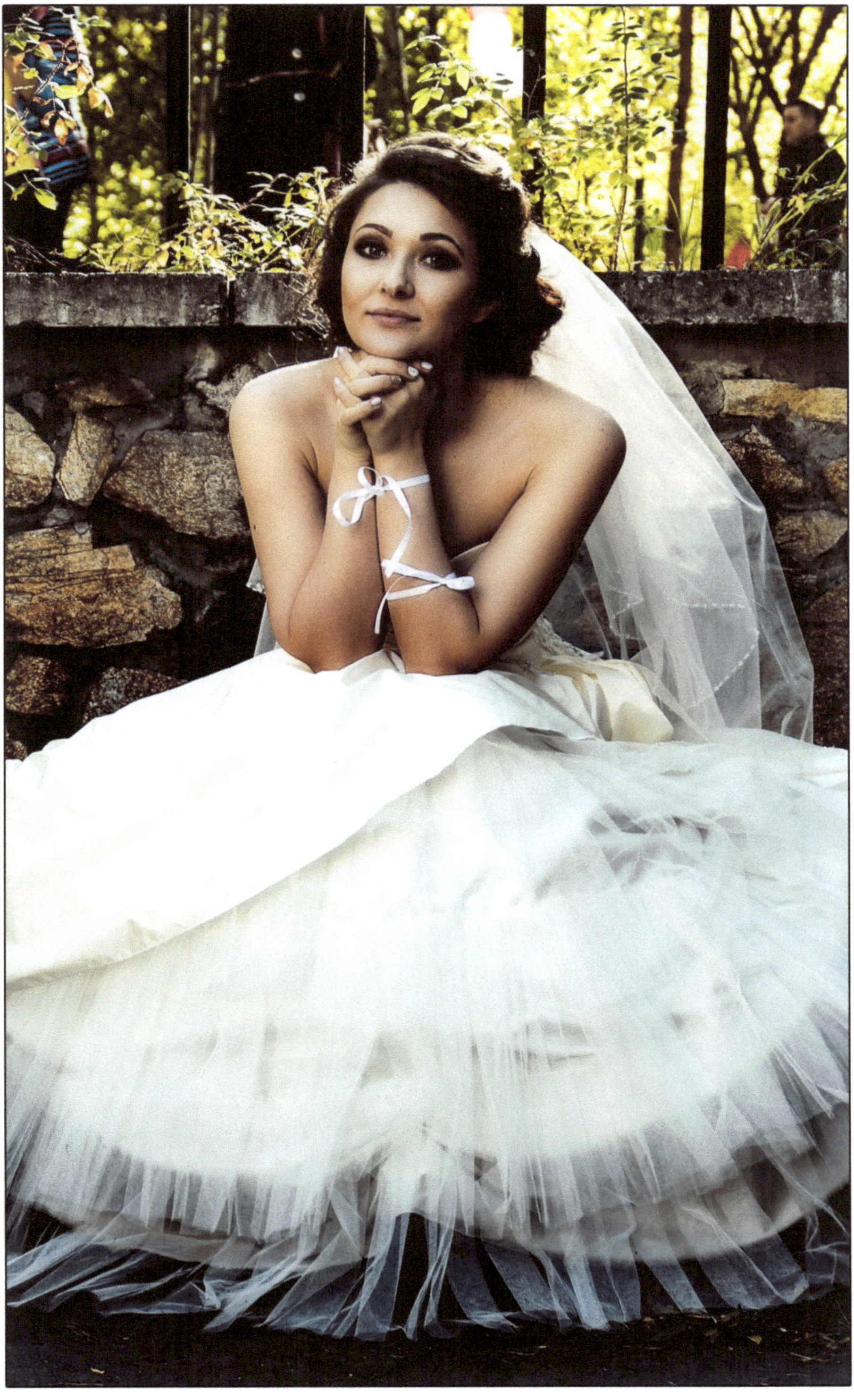

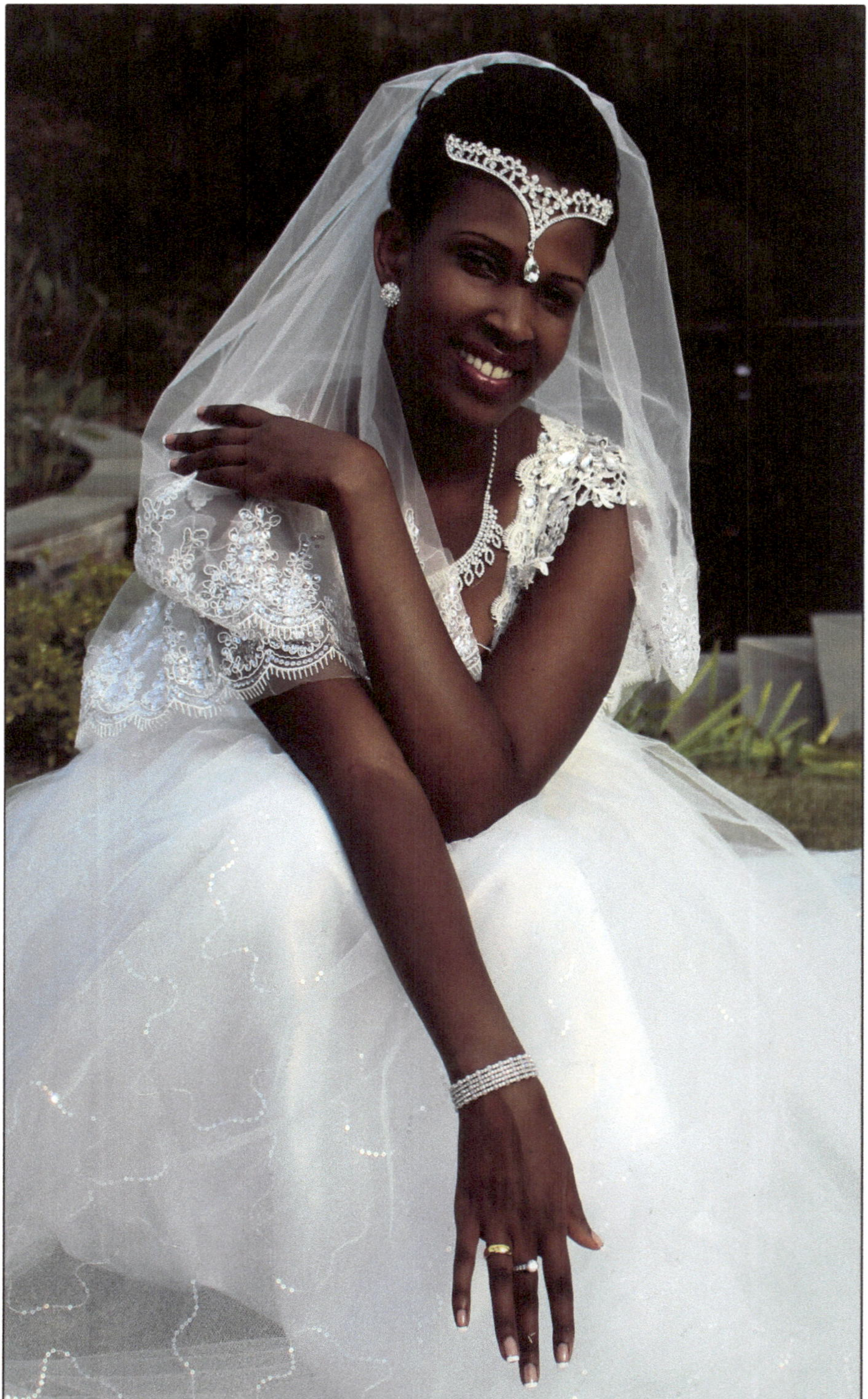

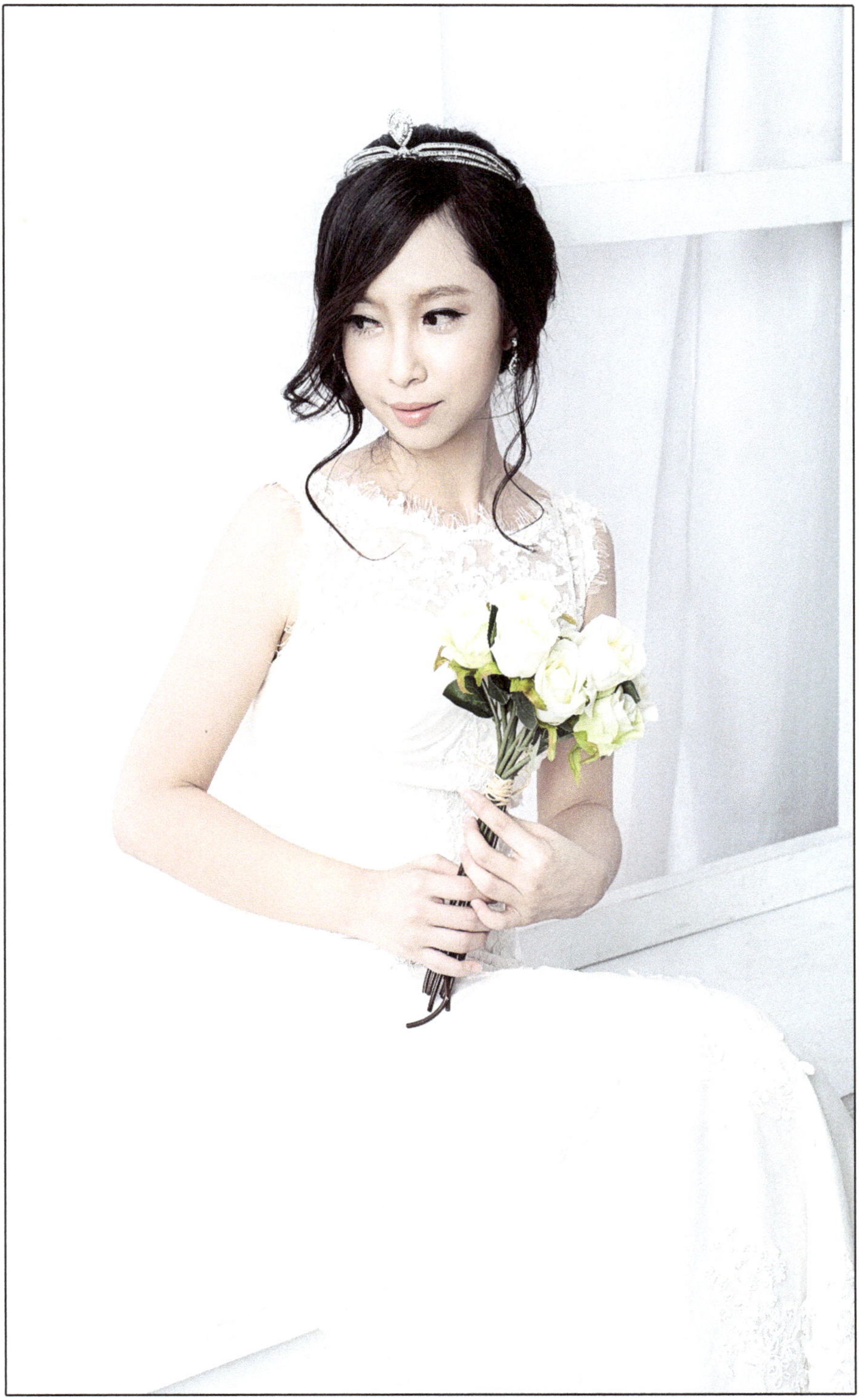

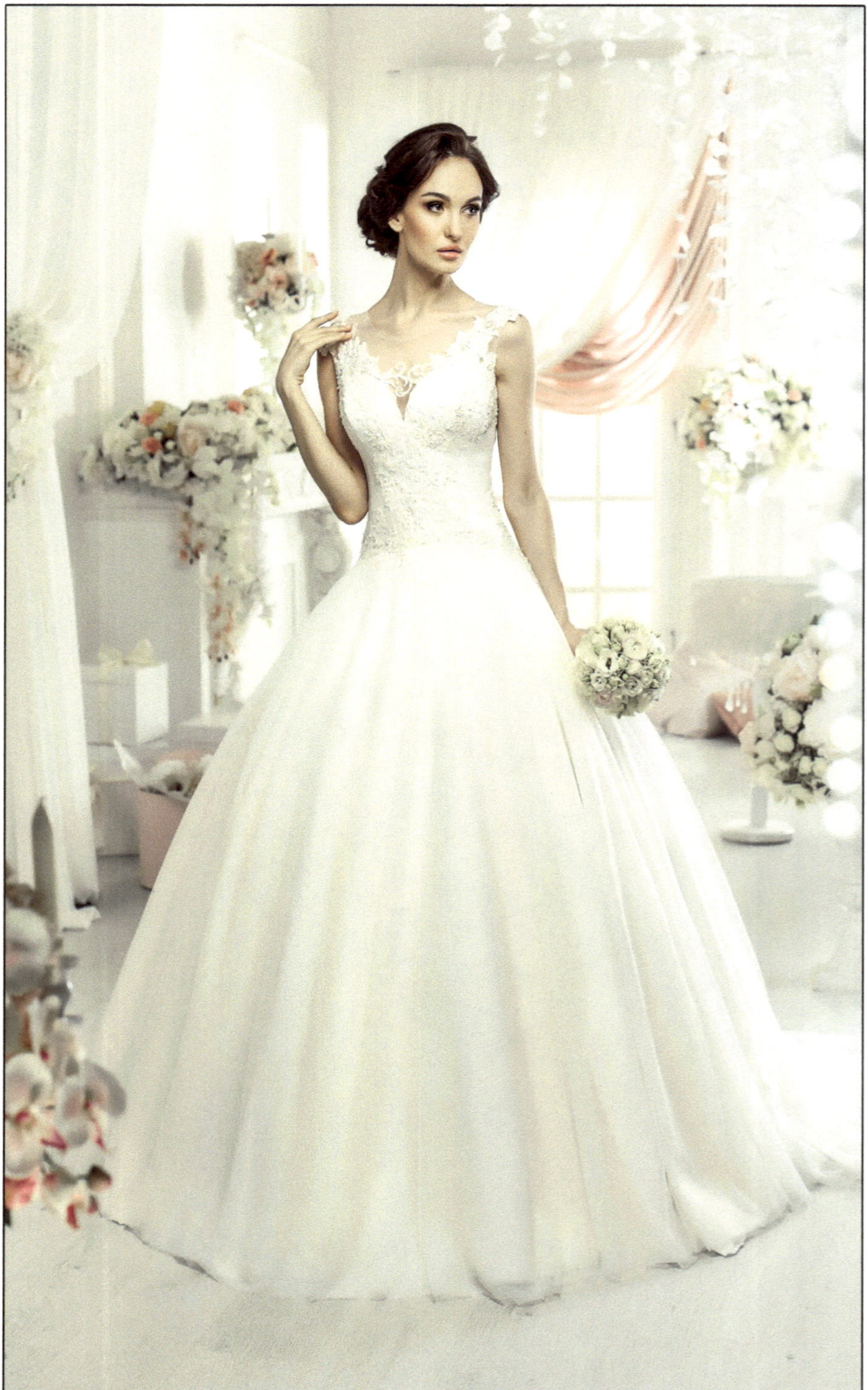

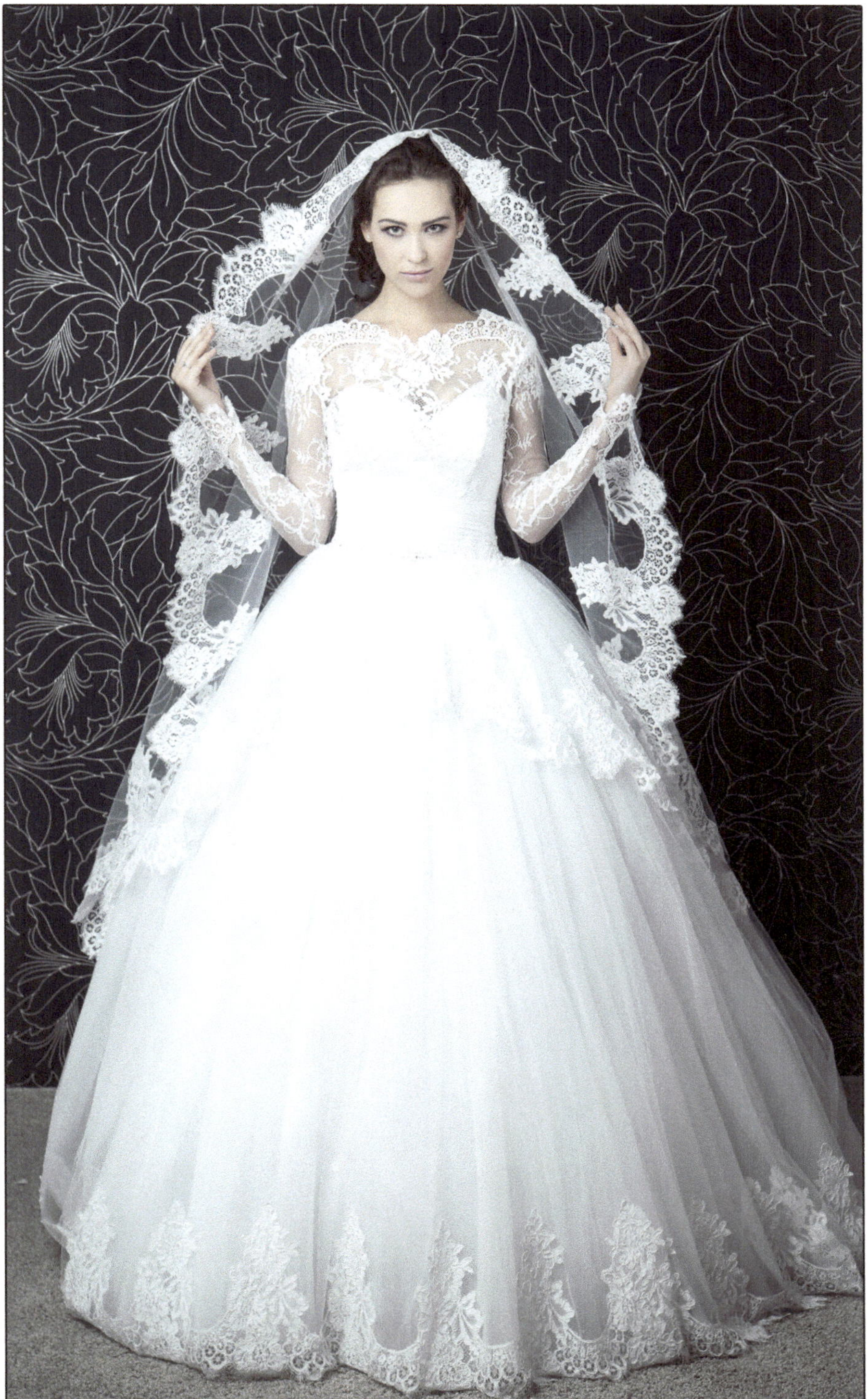

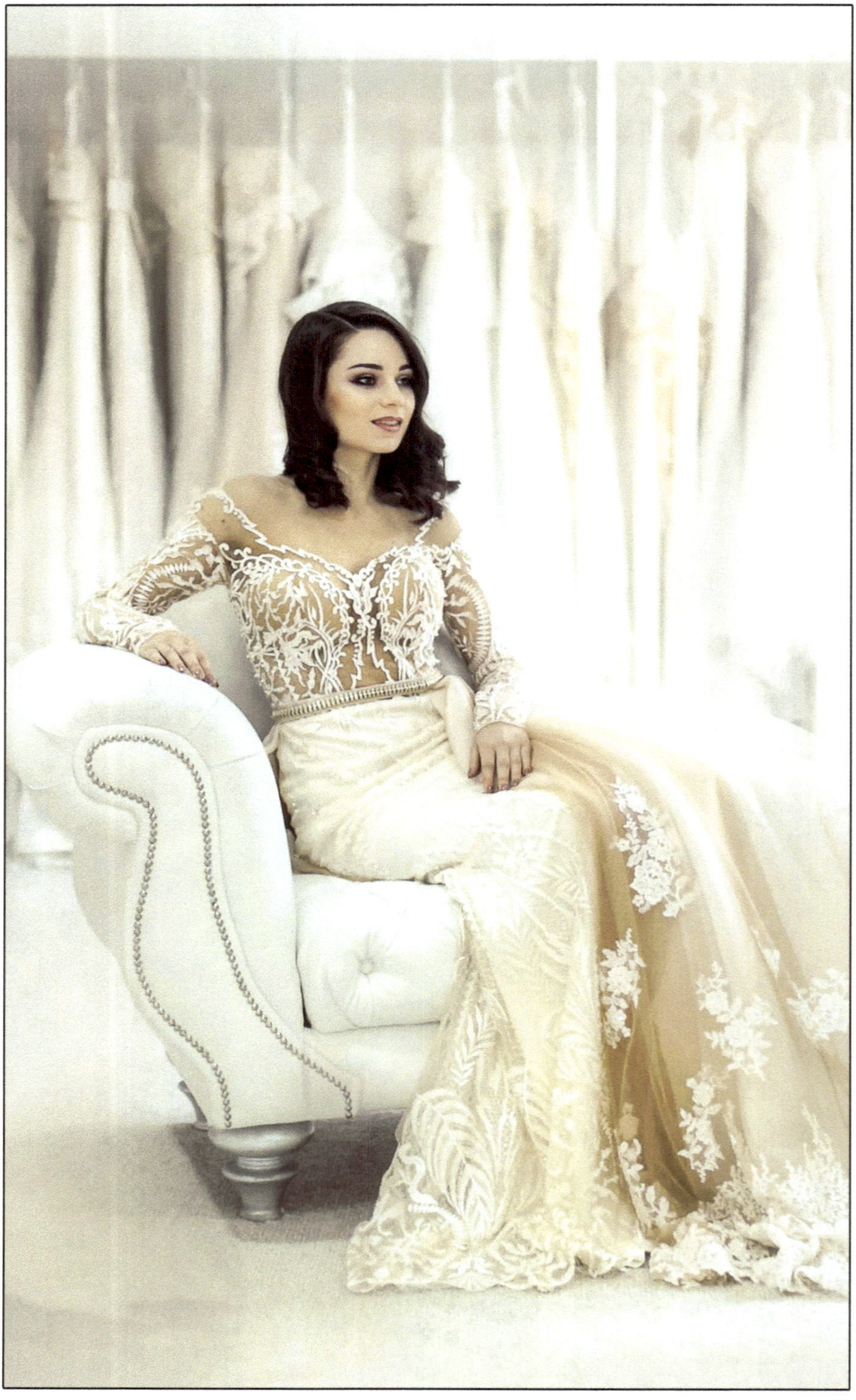

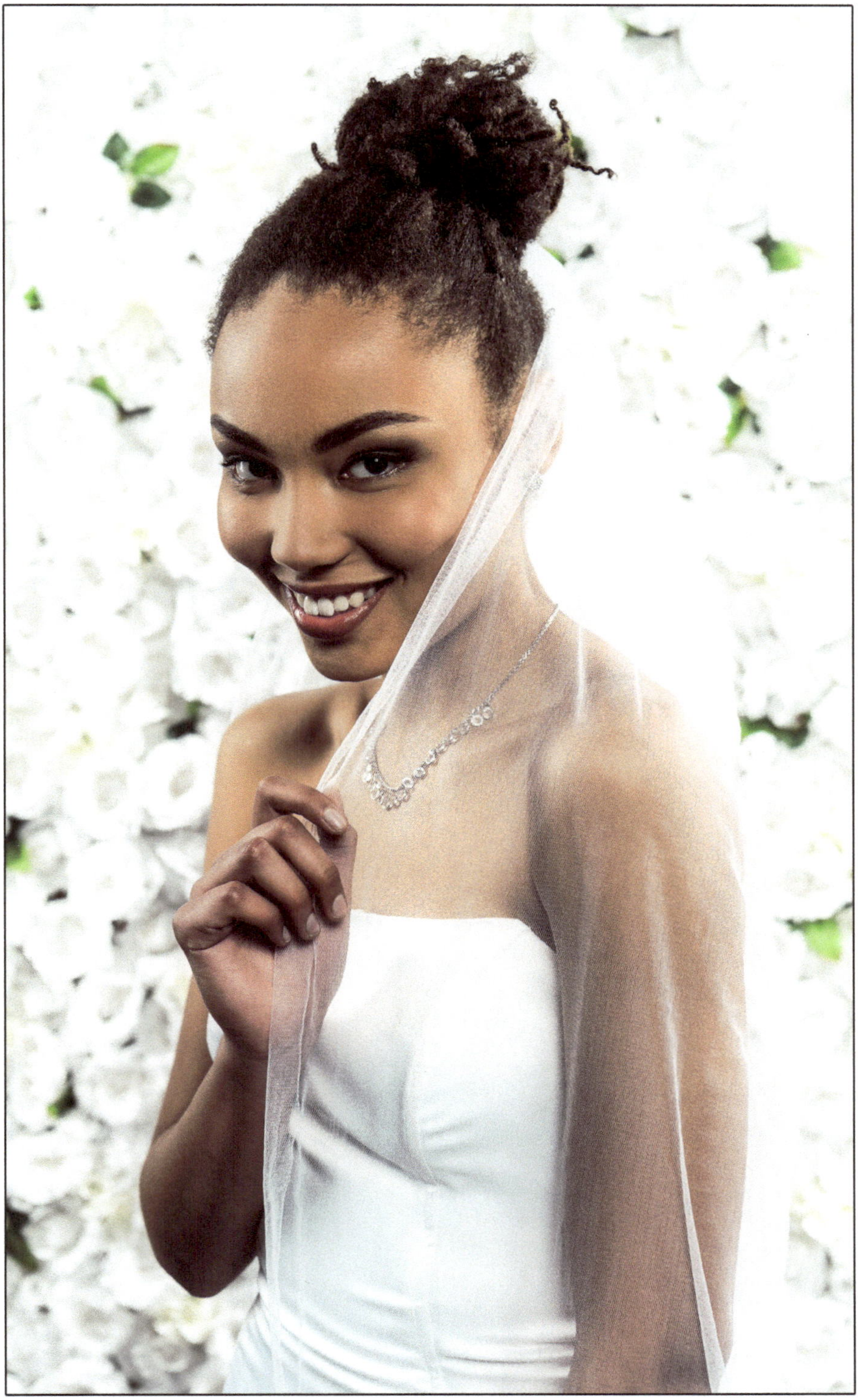

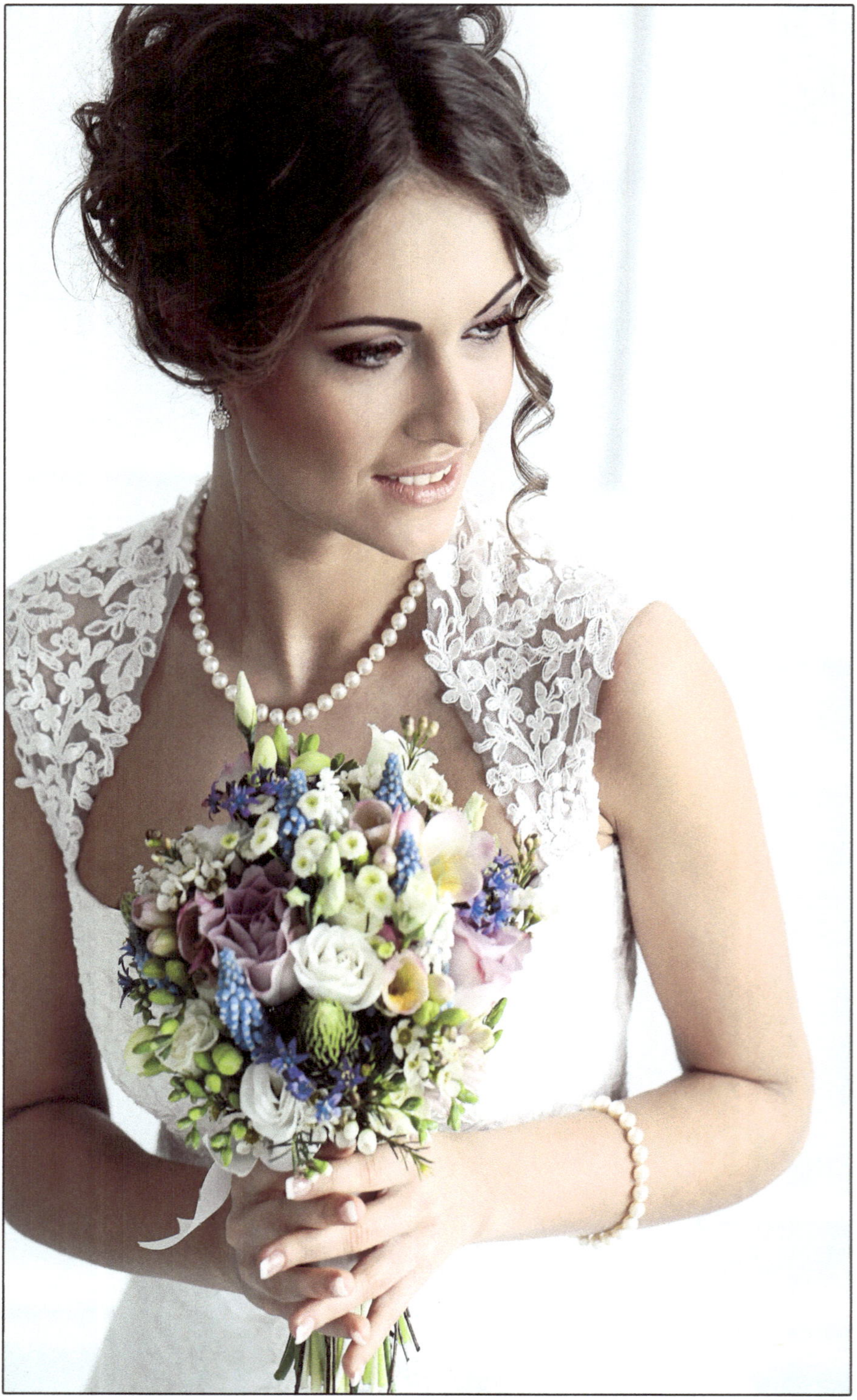

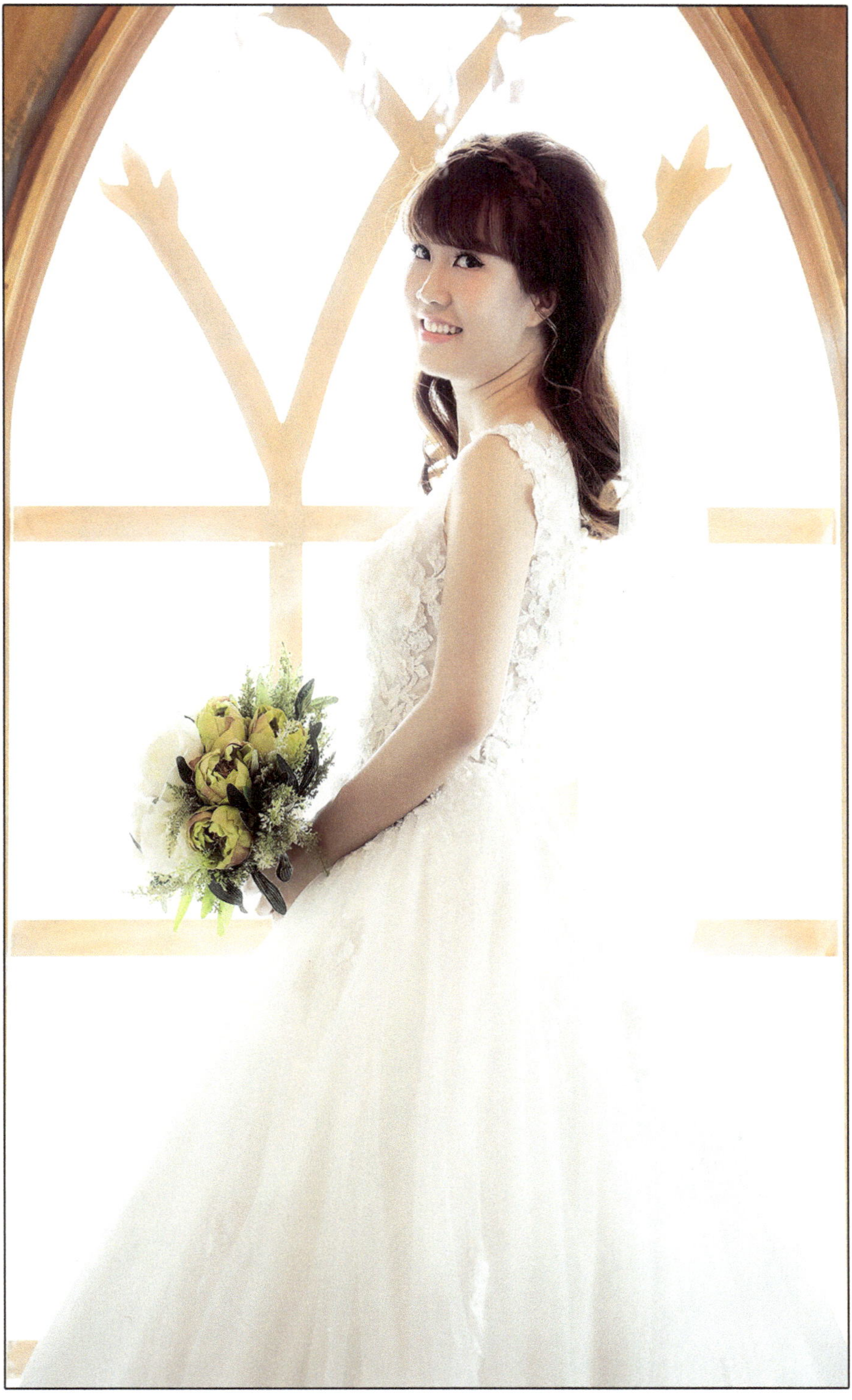

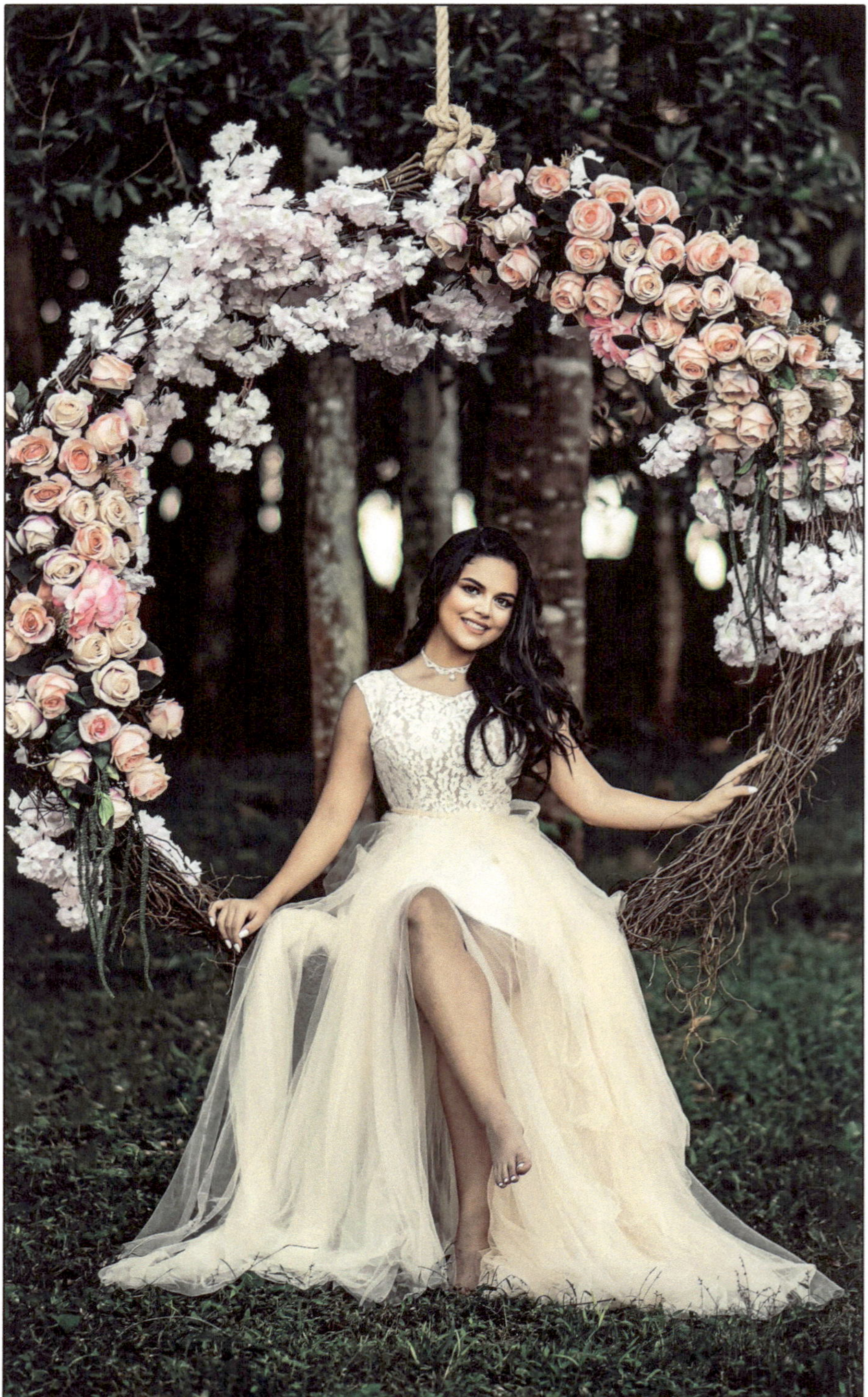

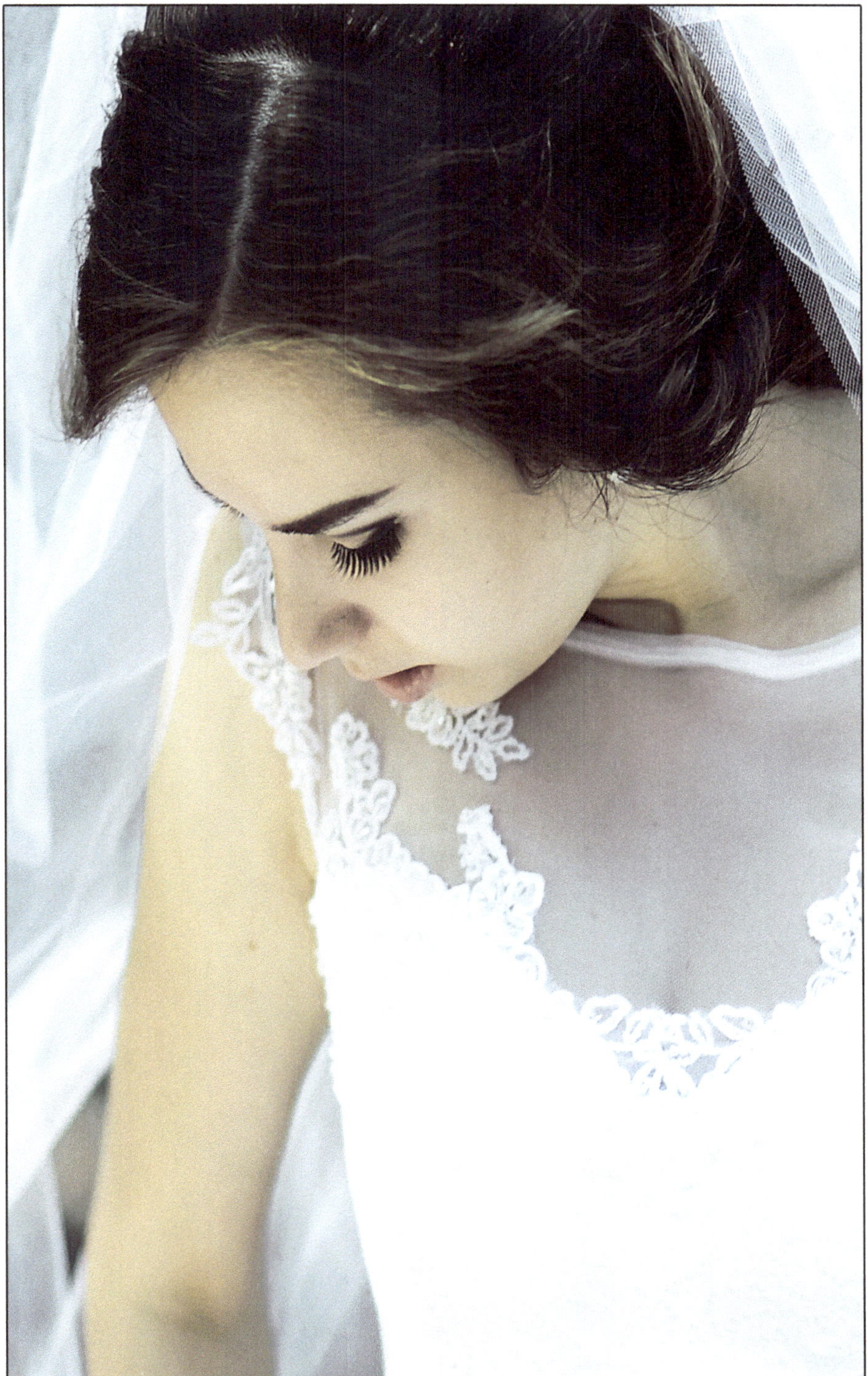

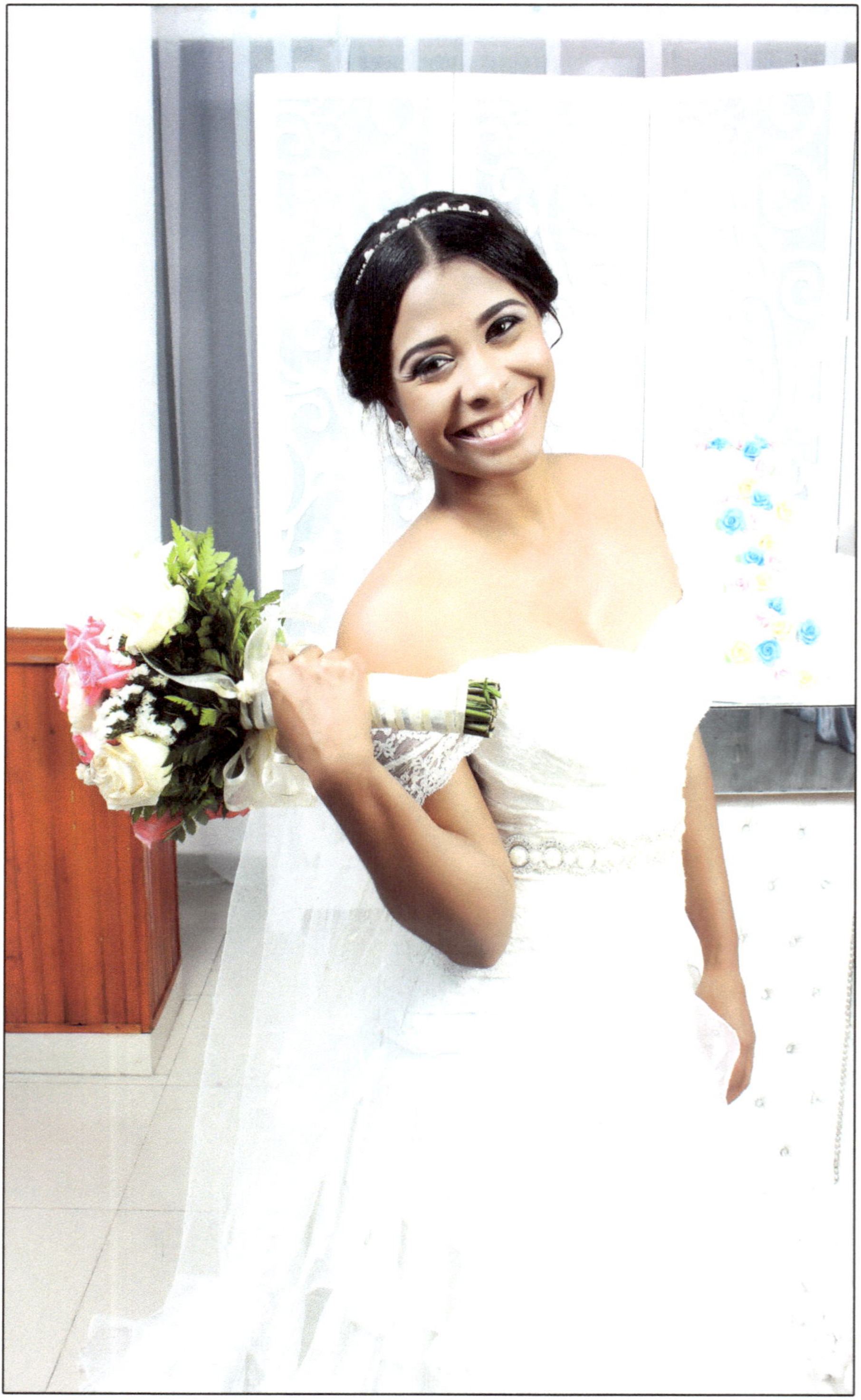

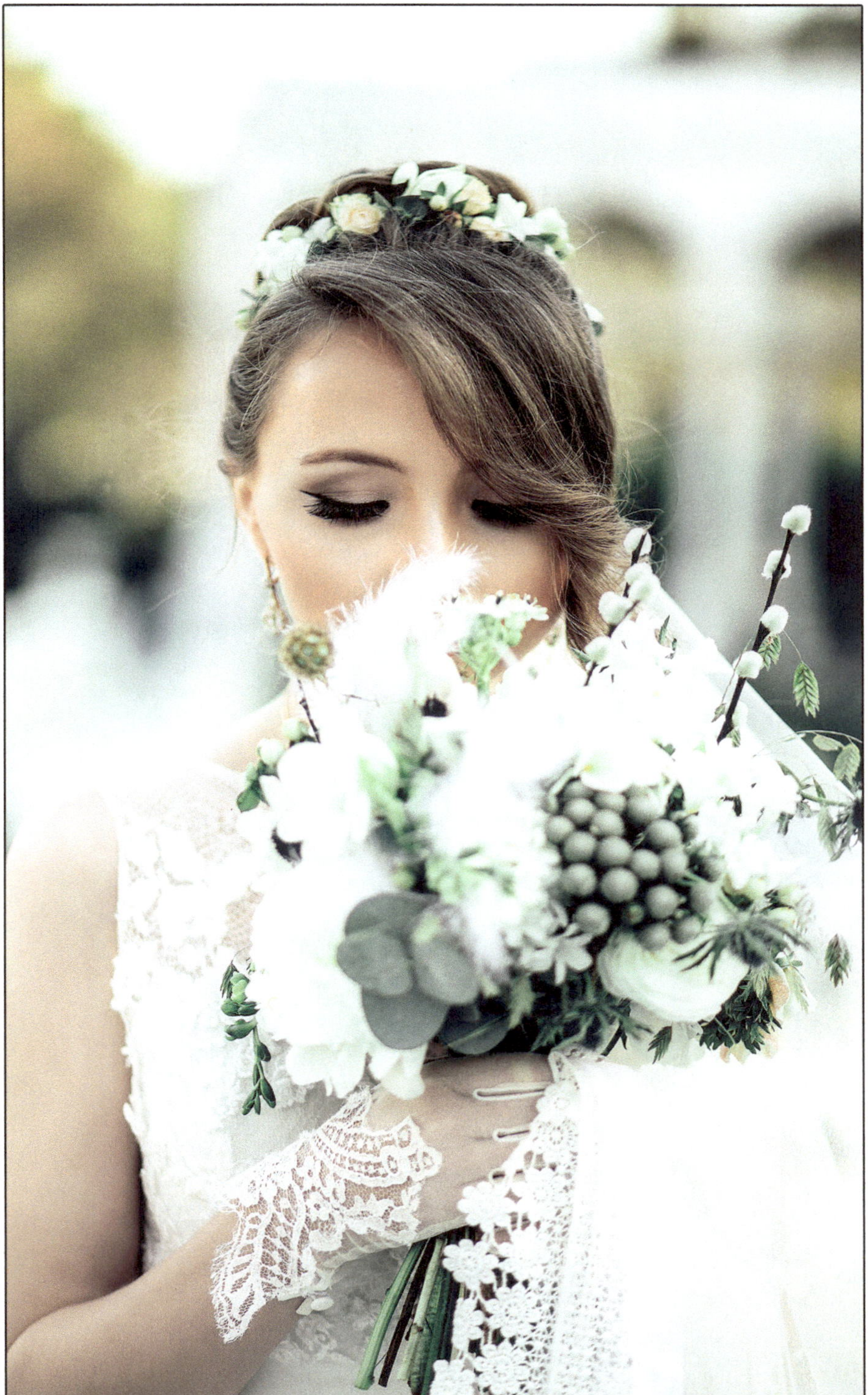

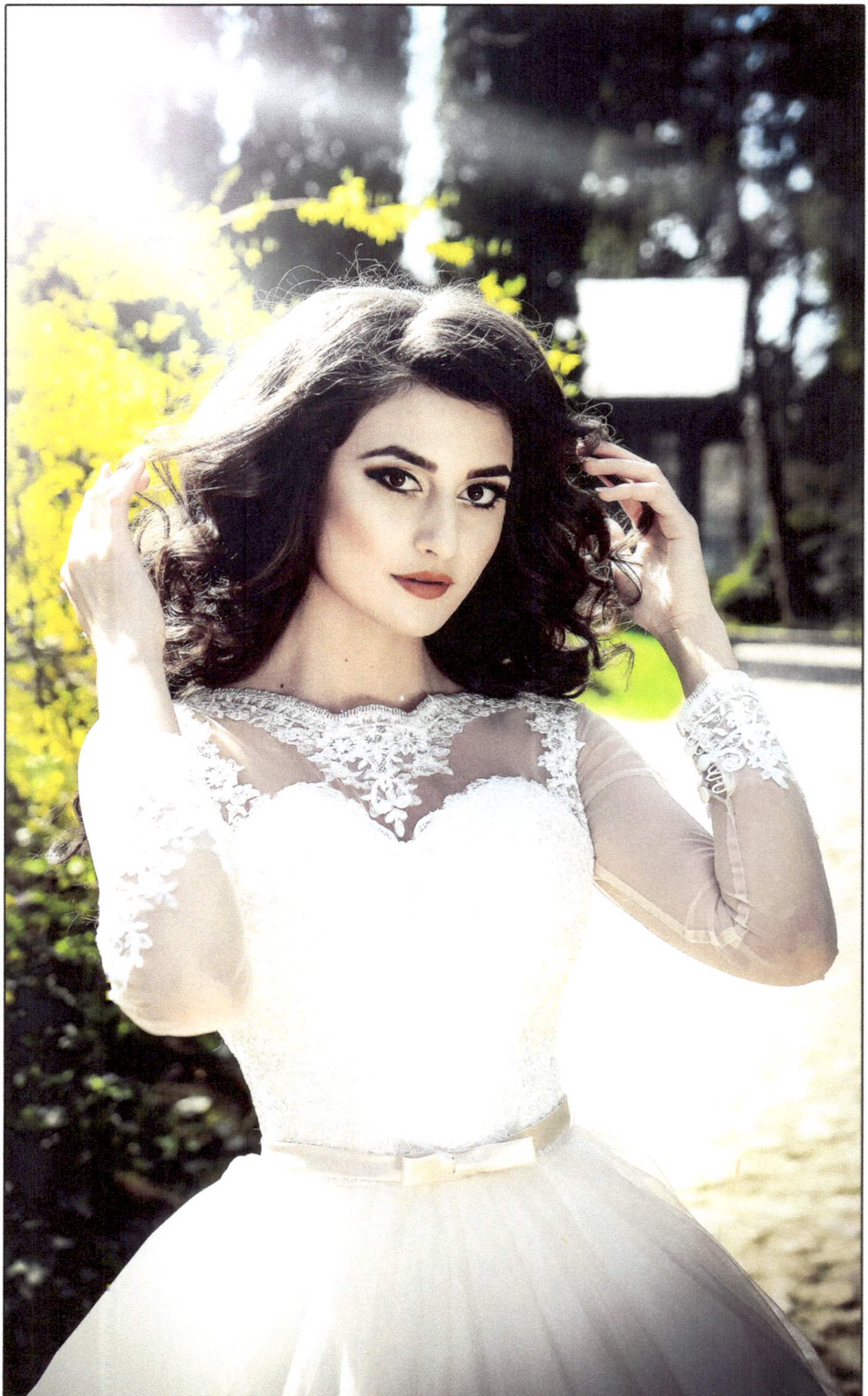

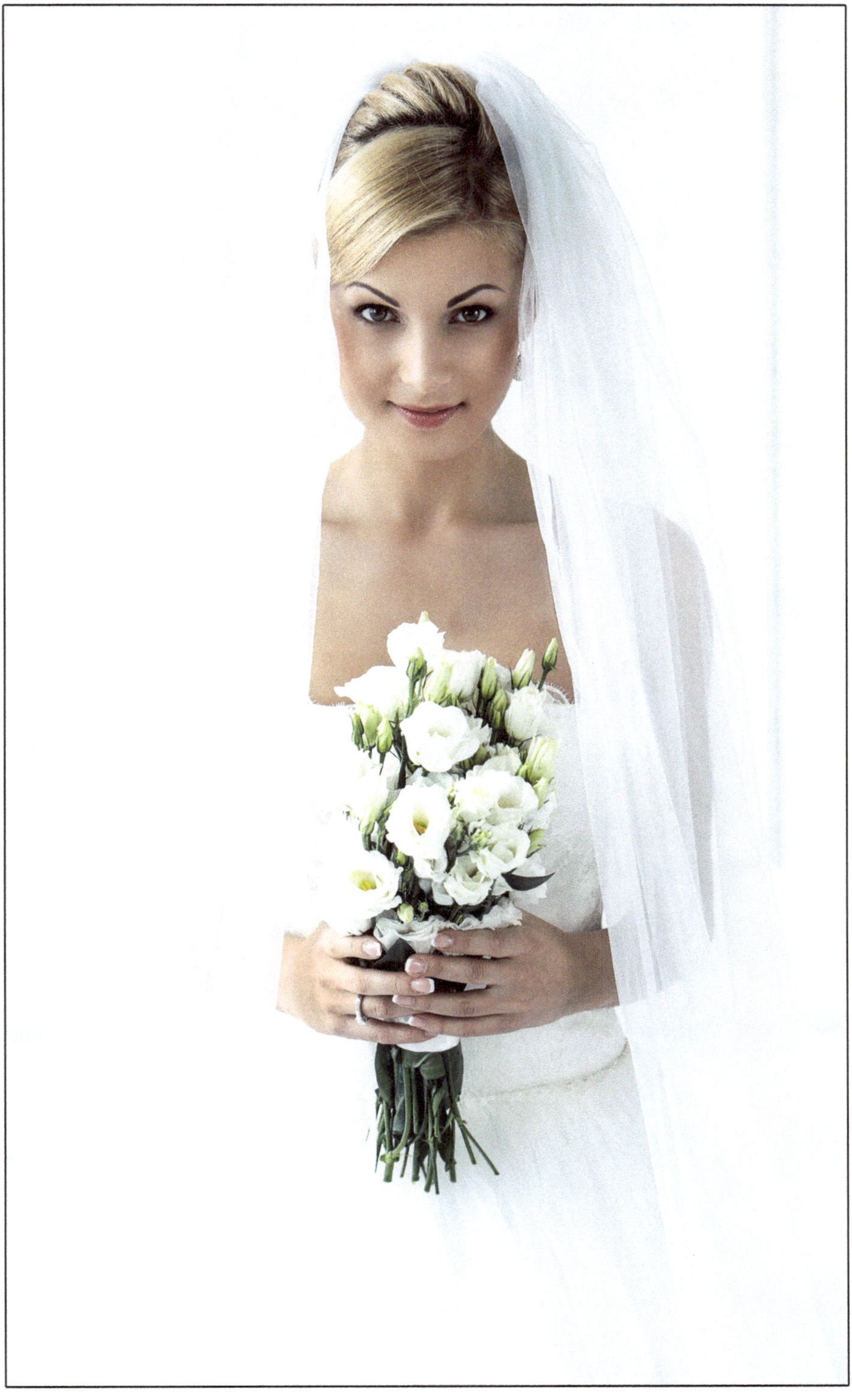

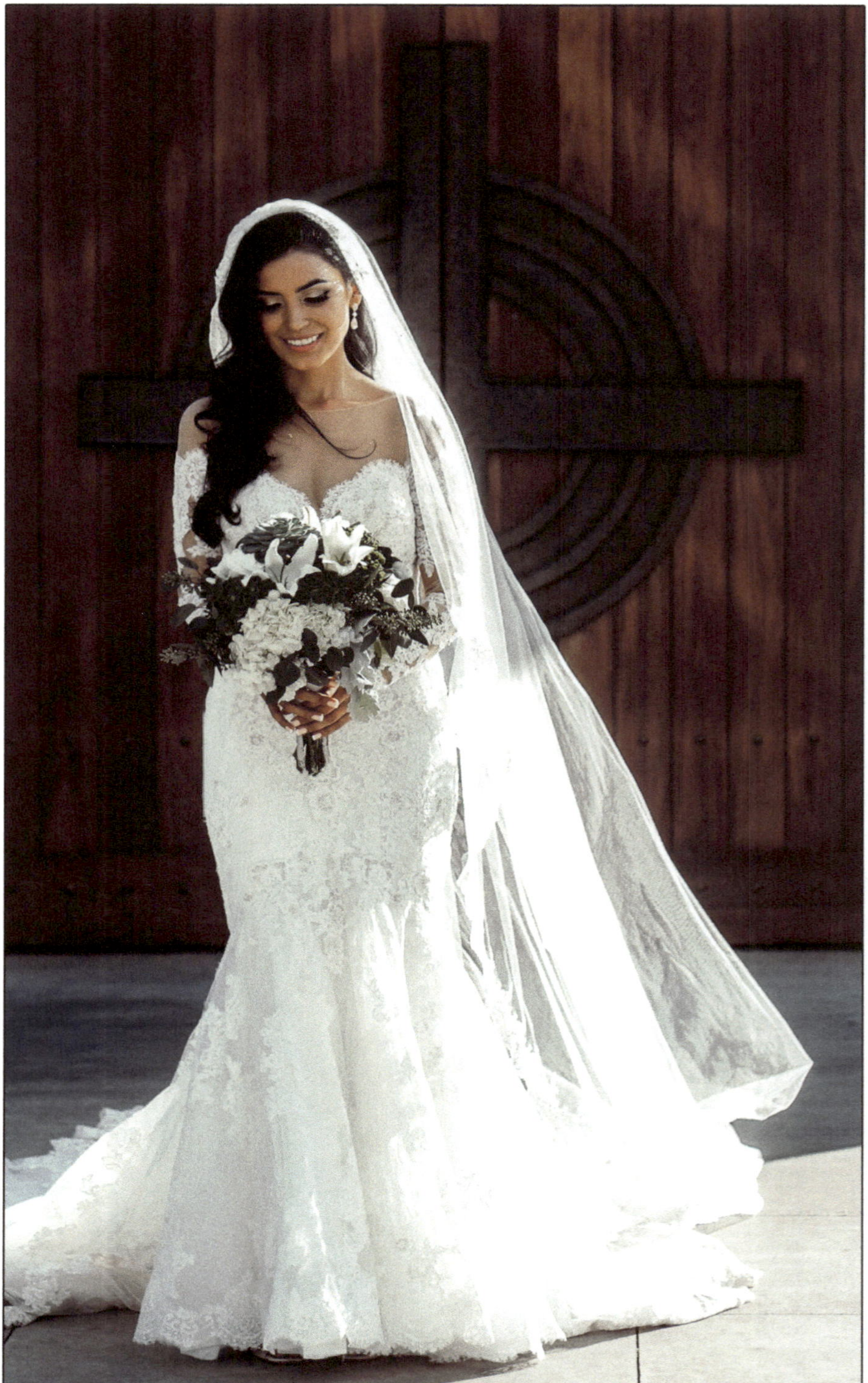

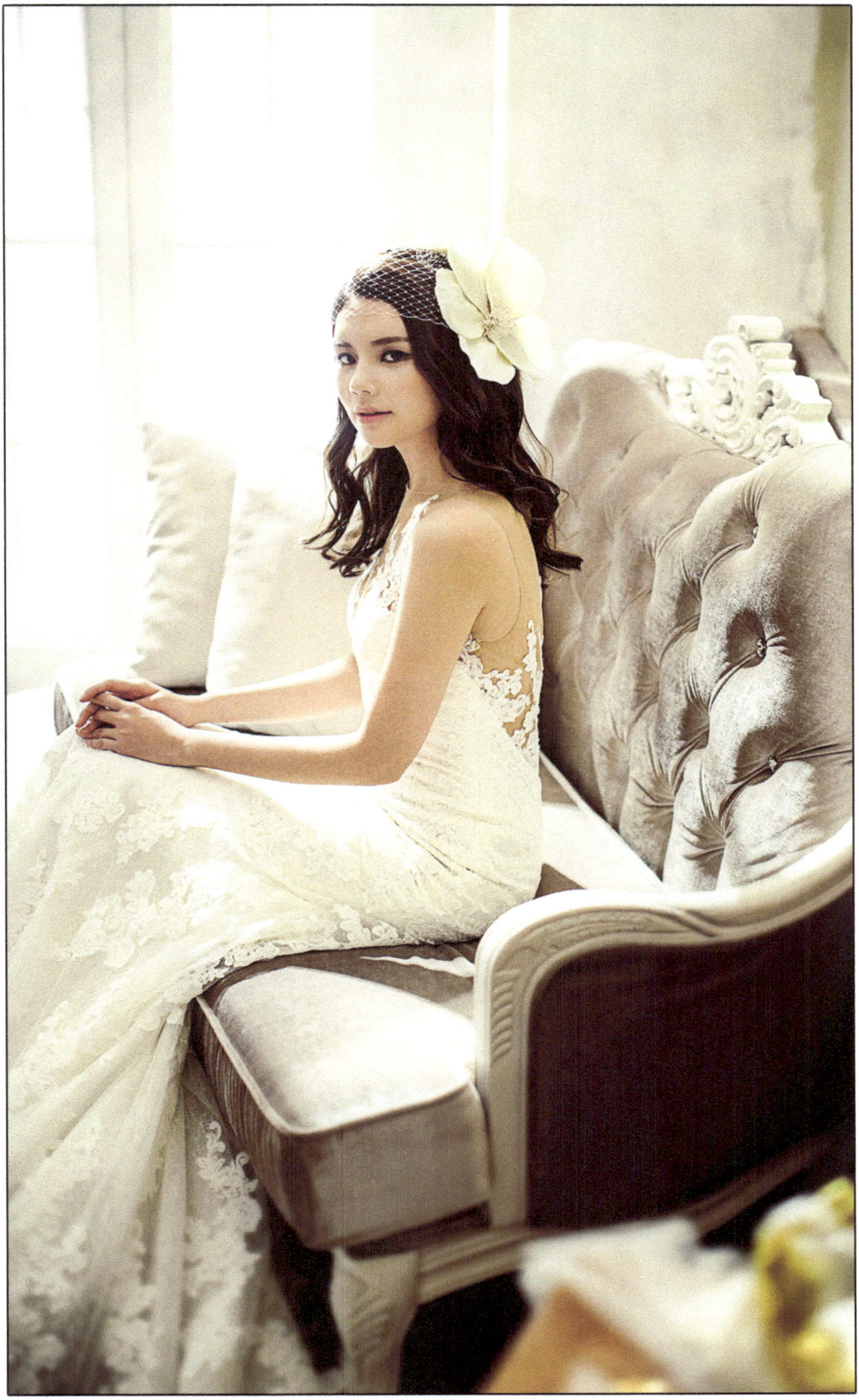

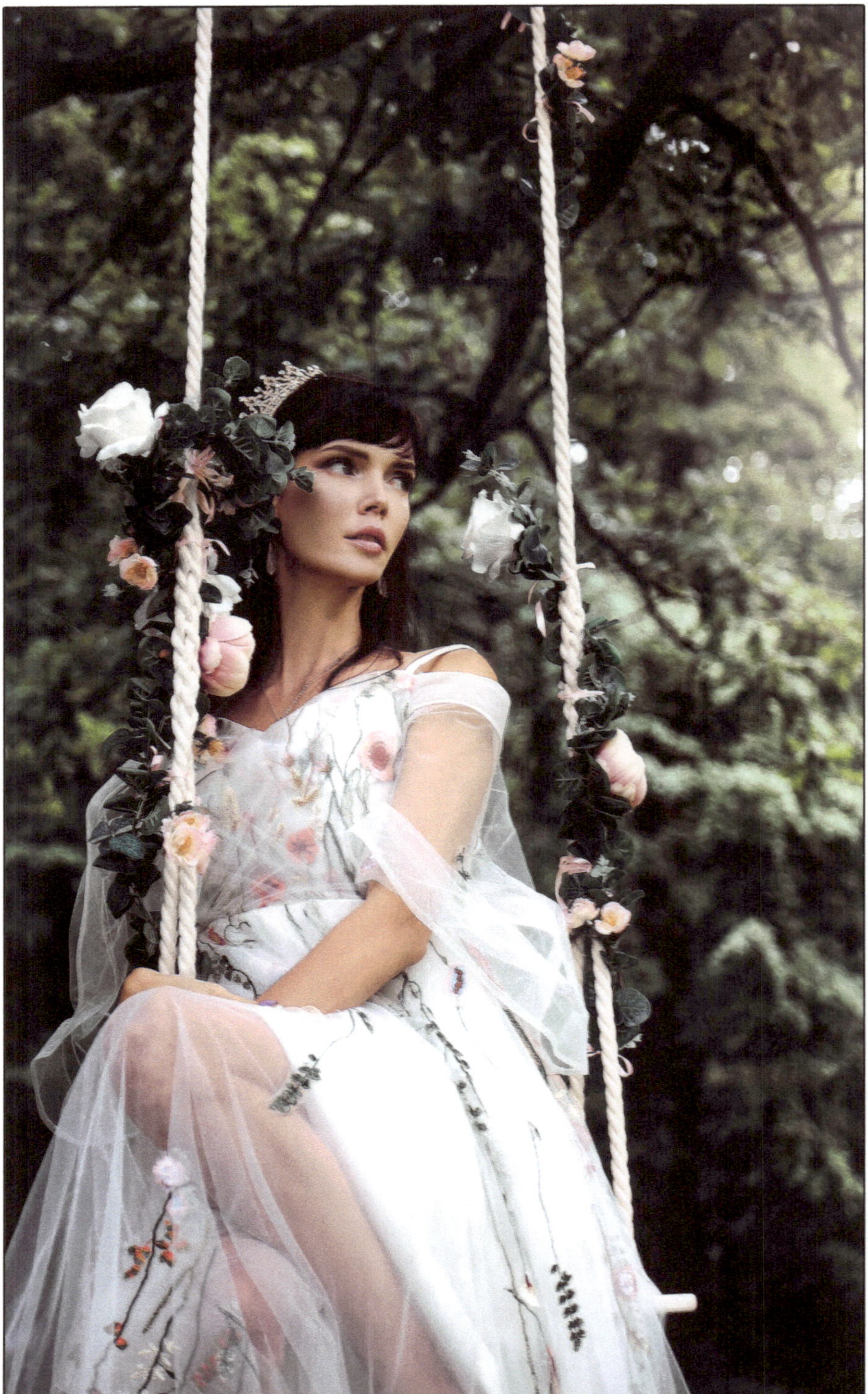

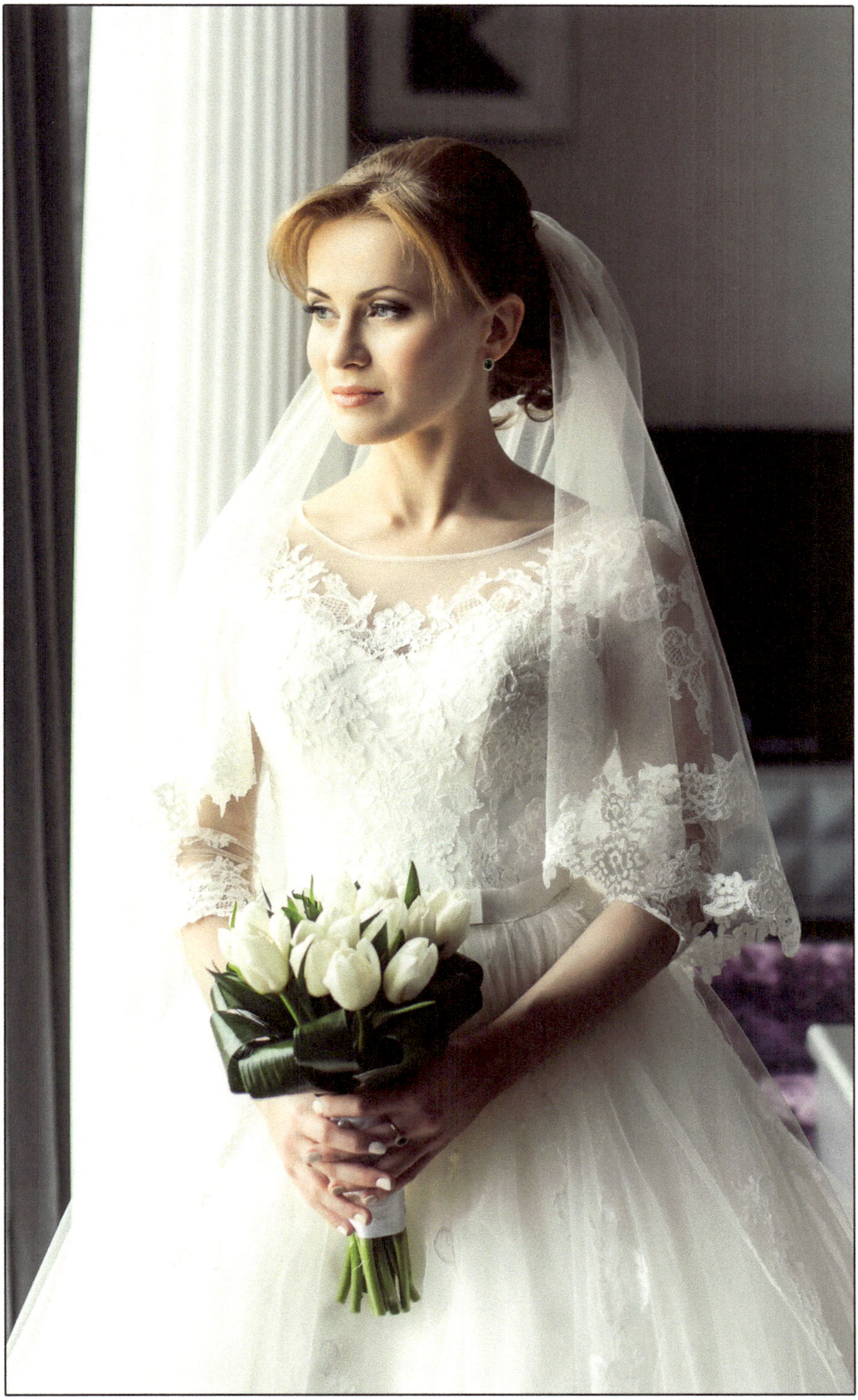

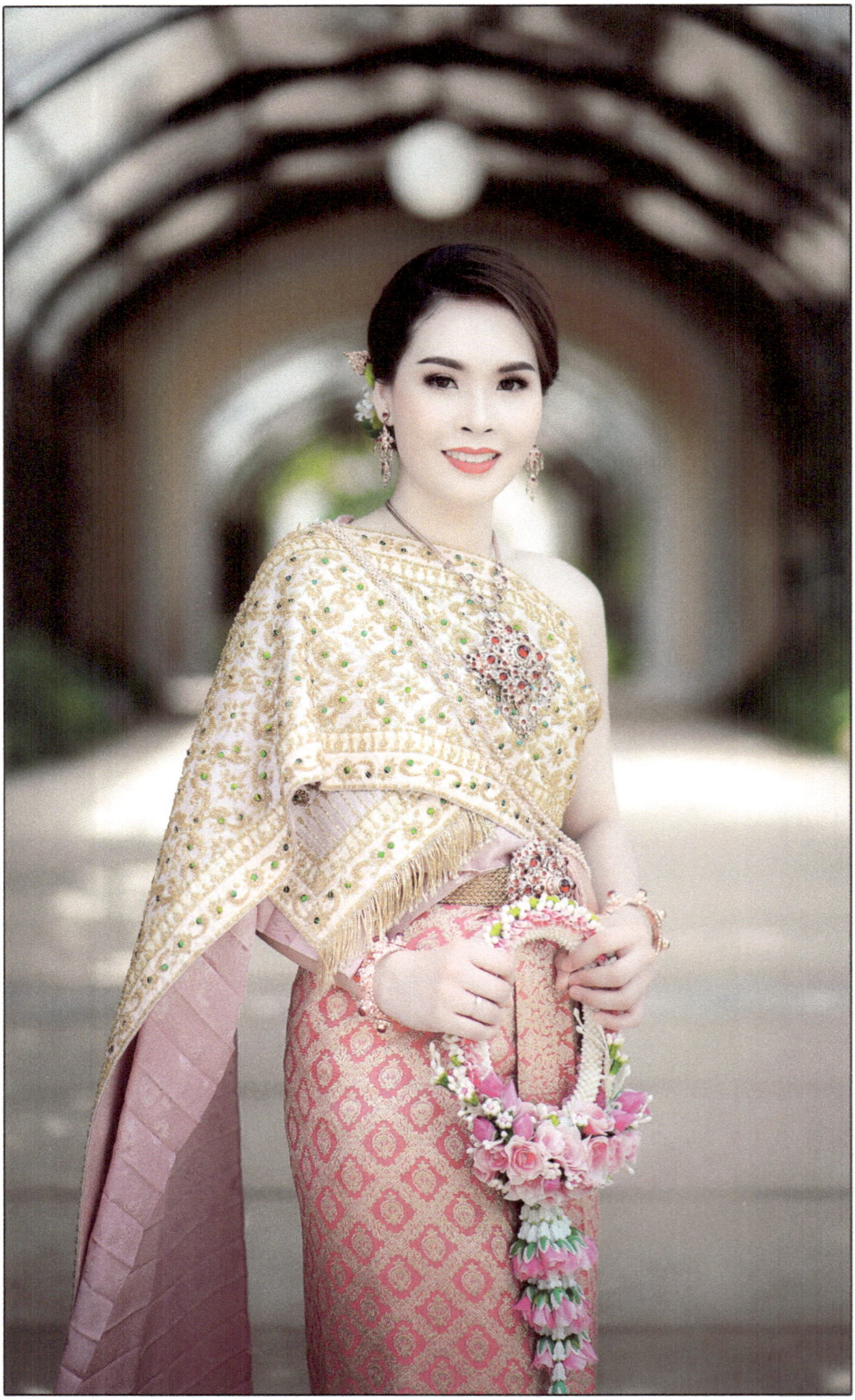

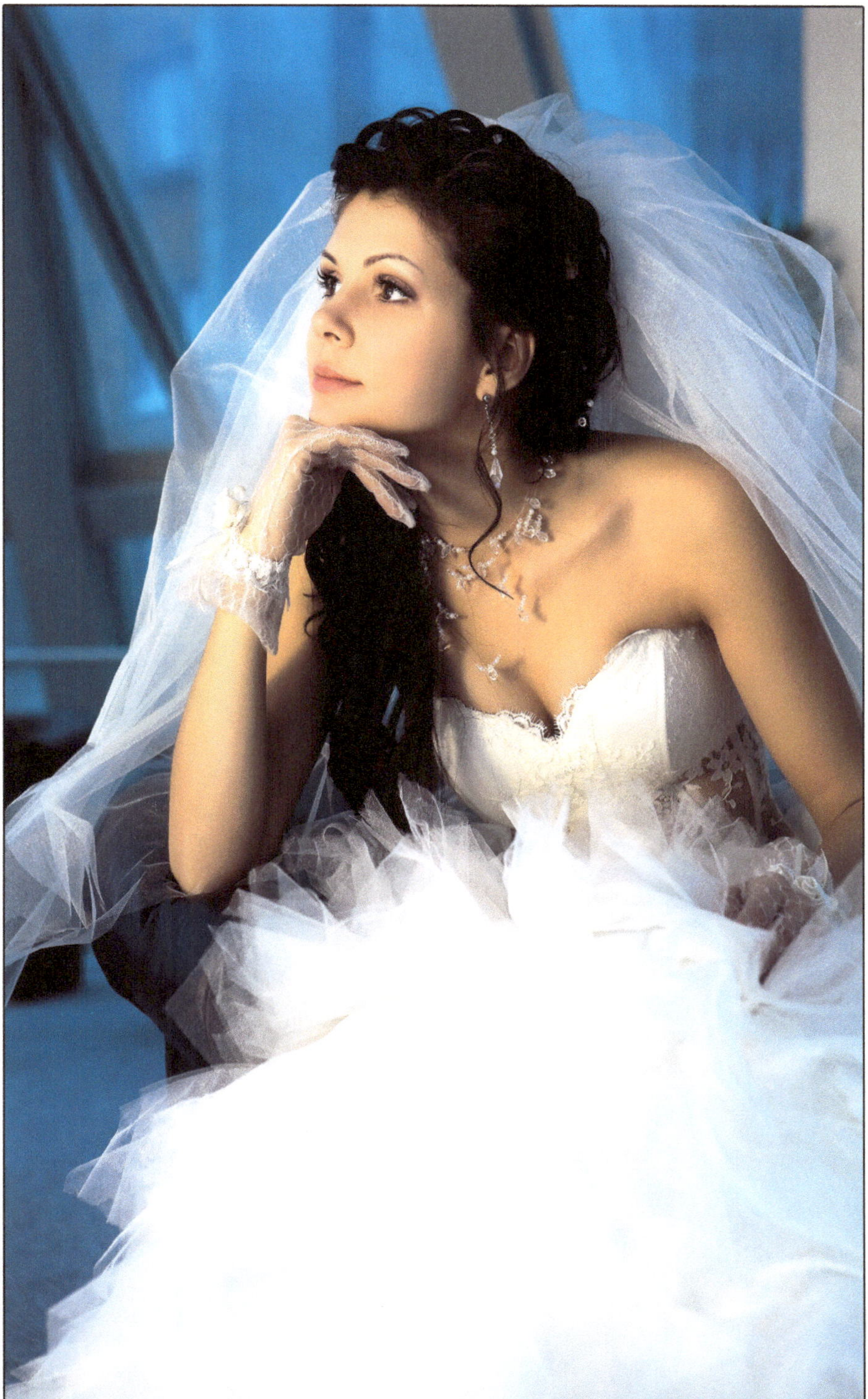

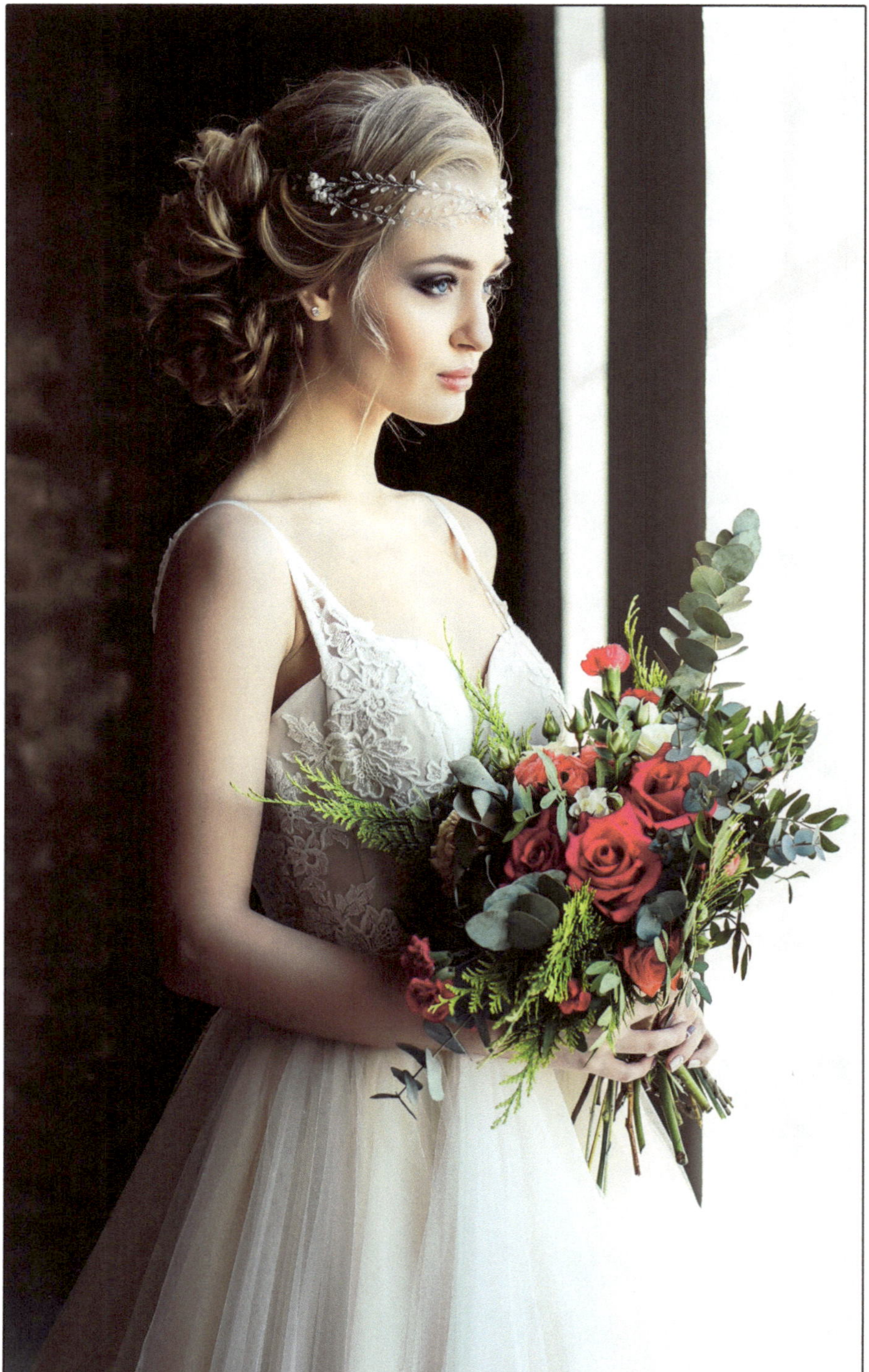

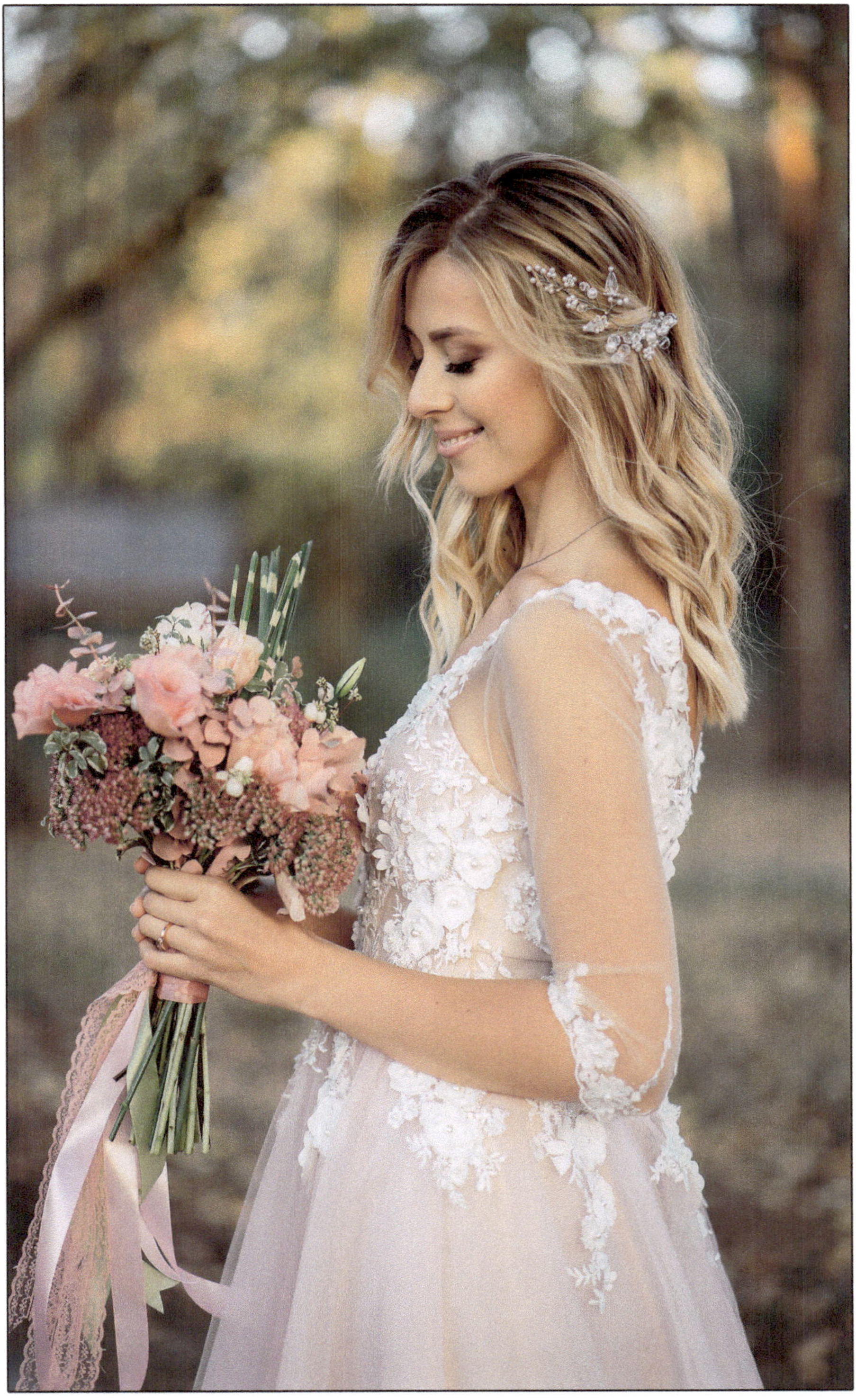

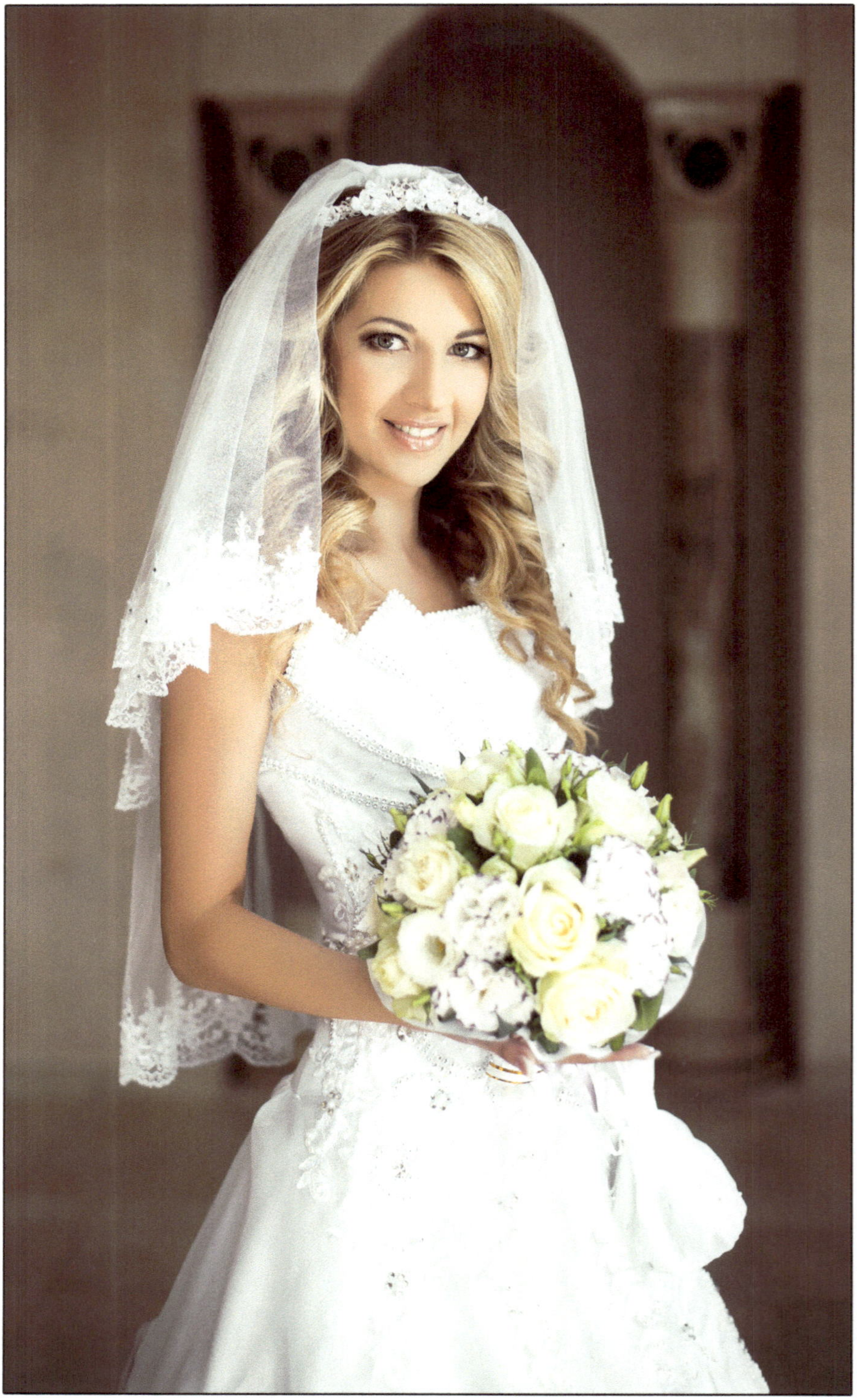

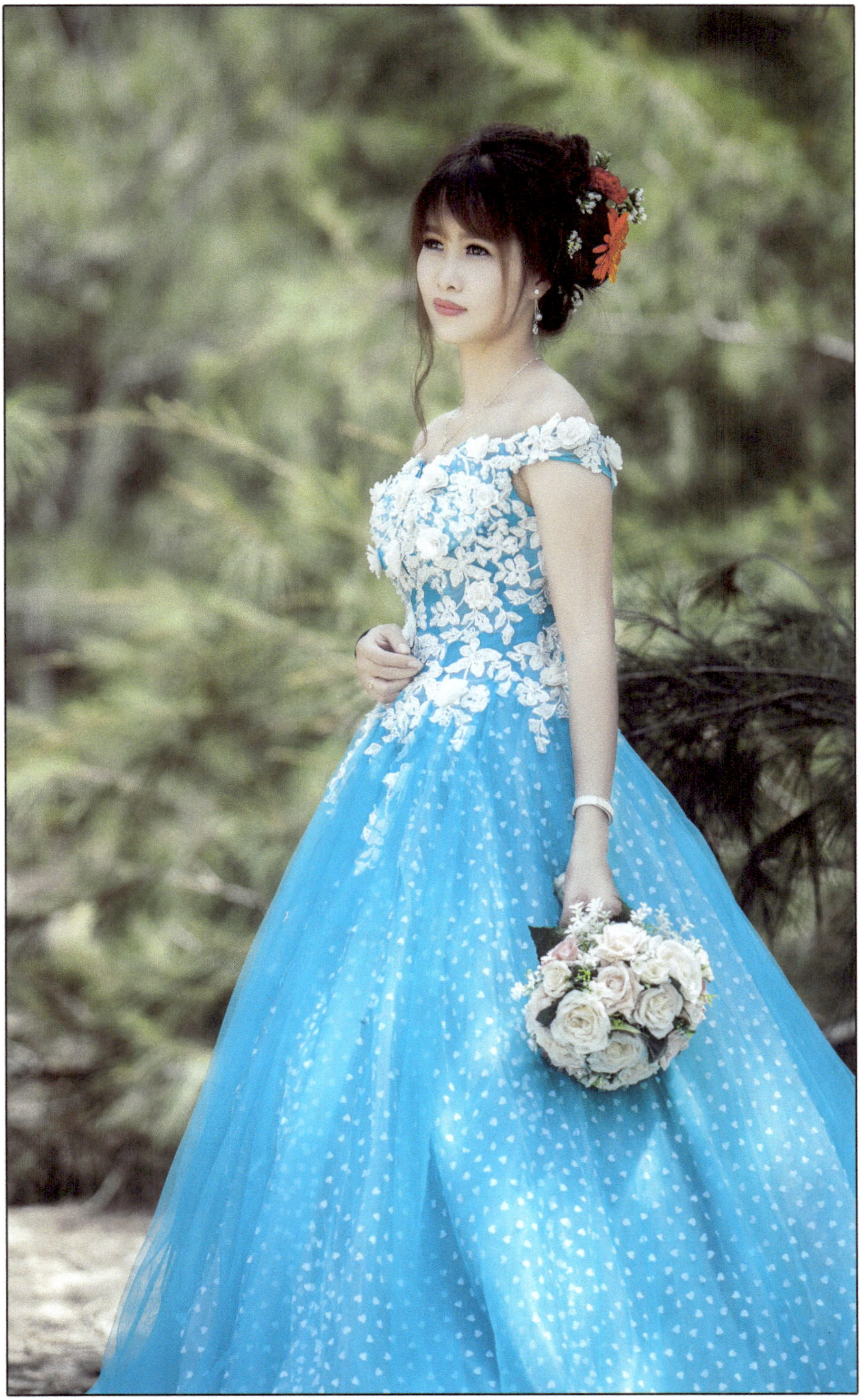

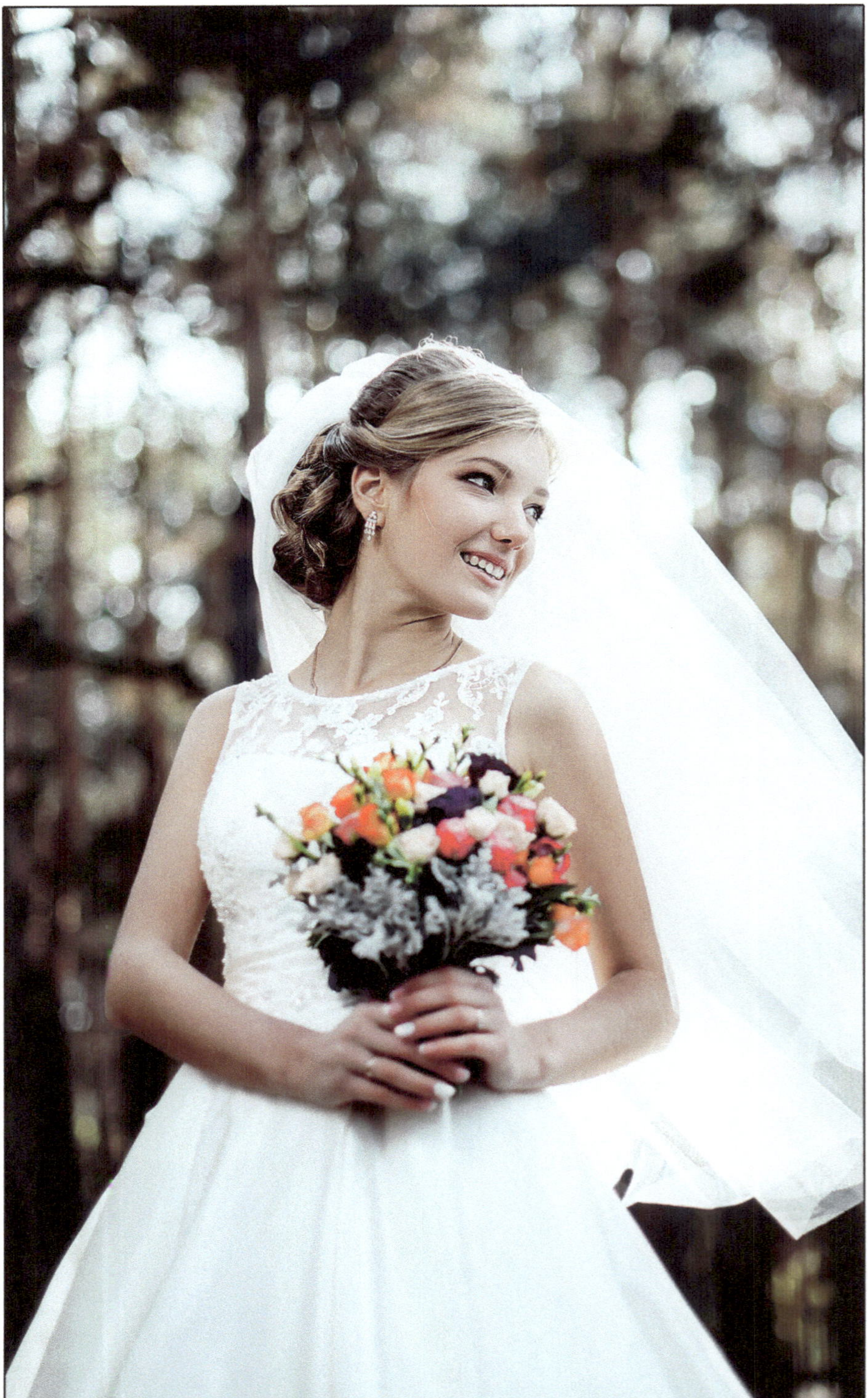

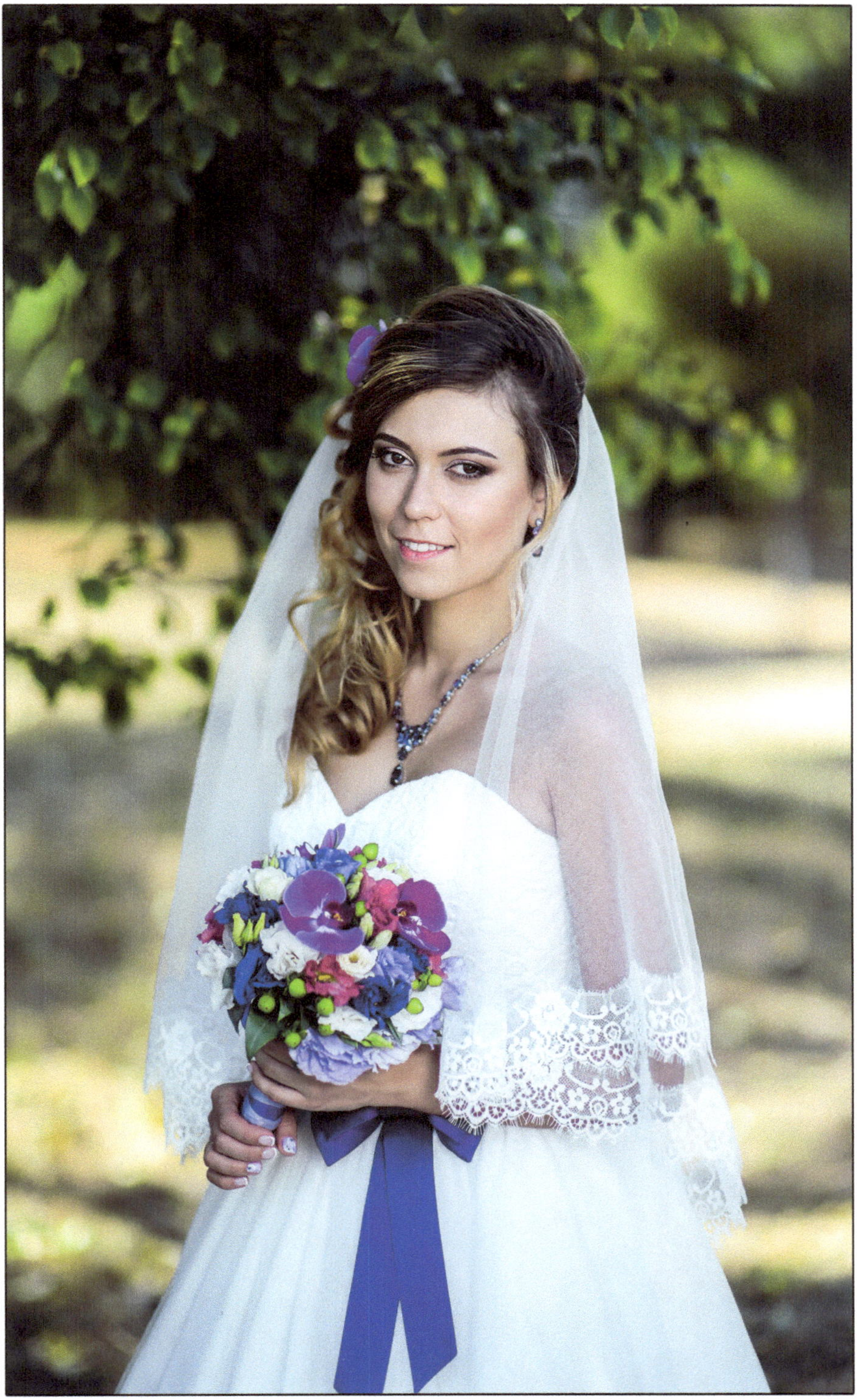

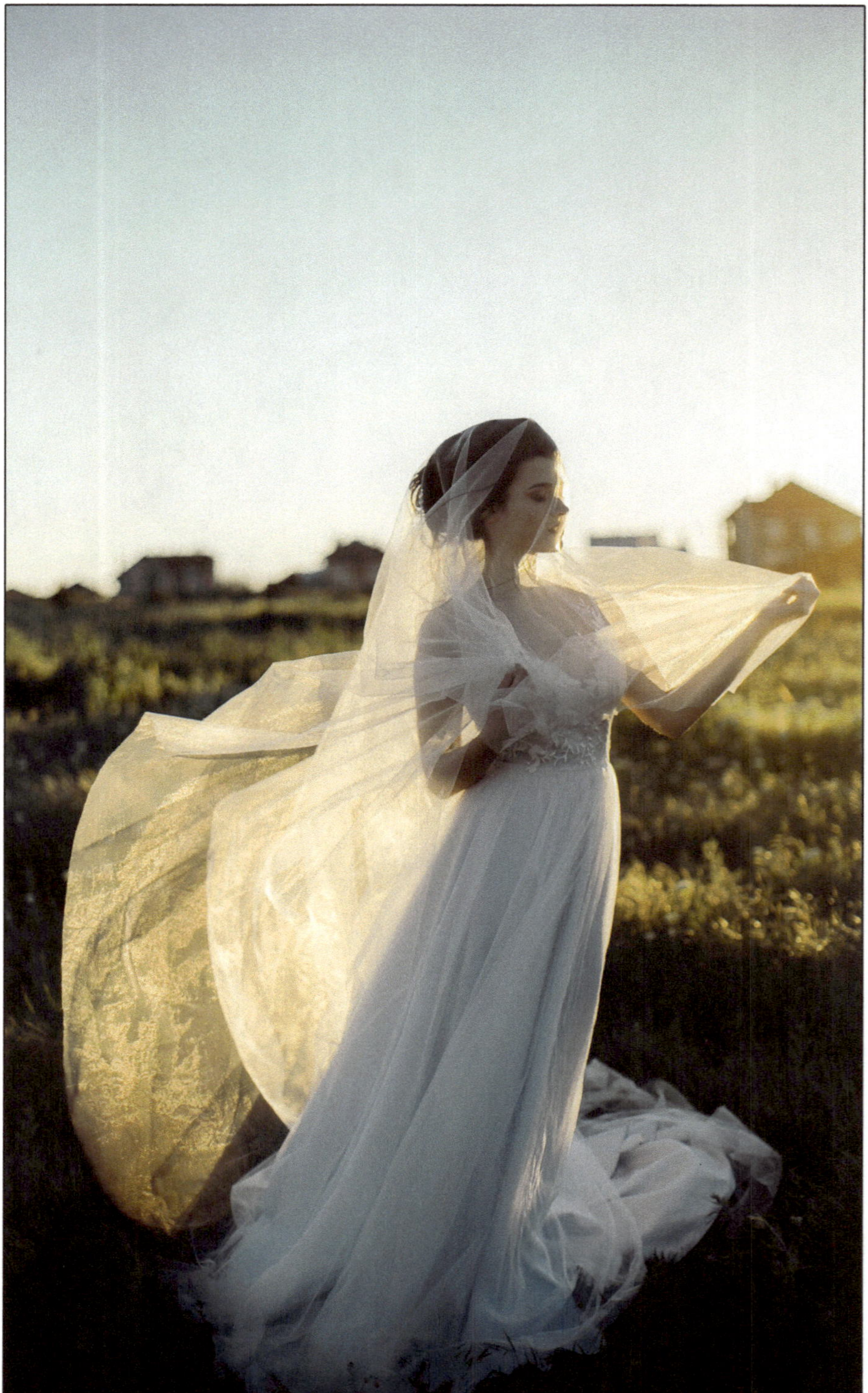

www.ingramcontent.com/pod-product-compliance
Lightning Source LLC
Chambersburg PA
CBHW050757290526
45792CB00008B/2216
* 9 7 8 1 0 8 9 5 0 4 2 1 4 *